GUIDE TO

ADVENTURE SPORTS

UK UNITED KINGDOM

All about them, how to do them, where to go

EMMA DREW & IRVINE CONNER

GUIDE TO
ADVENTURE
SPORTS
All about them, how to do them, where to go
EMMA DREW & IRVINE CONNER
UK
UNITED KINGDOM

First published 2007 by
A & C Black Publishers Ltd
38 Soho Square, London W1D 3HB
www.acblack.com

ISBN-13: 978 0 7136 8149 9

A CIP catalogue record for this book is available from the British Library.

Note: While every effort has been made to ensure the content of this book is as technically accurate and as sound as possible, neither the author nor the publishers can accept responsibility for any injury or loss sustained as a result of the use of this material.

Cover design by Steve Russell
Text design by James Watson

Front cover photograph of kiteboarder © Getty Images/Photographer's Choice/Karl Weatherly
Back cover photographs courtesy of www.istockphoto.com

Inside photographs courtesy of the following: Team Elan, Andy Wright p. 43; Corbis/zefa (Hein van den Heuvel) p. 93; Duncan Eades p. 153; EMPICS pp. 143 (Adam Davy), 100 (Mike Egerton); EMPICS/AP pp. 18 (Dmitry Lovetsky), 35 (Maurice McDonald), 37 (Neil Munns), 160 (Rob Griffith); EMPICS/PA (Jane Mingay) p. 111; EMPICS/Scanpix (Thomas Bjornflaten); John Welch, Flight Culture p. 2; Lee Stone p. 149; Michael Comber pp. 87–8; PhotoDisc, Inc. pp. 103–4; Preseli Venture www.preseliventure.com pp. iii, 139; Rob Eavis Photography pp. 77–8; www.dropzoneuk.com p. 57; www.gerardbrown.co.uk pp. 68, 107; www.grahamheywood.co.uk p. xi; www.istockphoto.com pp. ix, 1, 4, 10, 22, 28, 50, 55, 59–60, 62–3, 71, 73, 82–3, 95, 114, 121–2, 125–6, 129–30, 135–6, 148, 157, 162–3, 170, 173, 175, 179, 181, 183–4; Zorb Ltd, New Zealand p. 119;

Colour photographs courtesy of the following: Team Elan, Andy Wright; EMPICS (Adam Davy), (Mike Egerton); EMPICS/AP (Christoph Ruckstuhl), (Dmitry Lovetsky), (Maurice McDonald), (Rob Griffith); John Welch; Michael Comber; PhotoDisc; Rob Eavis Photography; EMPICS/PA (Jane Mingay); EMPICS/Zuma Press; Preseli Venture www.preseliventure.com; www.dropzoneuk.com; www.gerardbrown.co.uk; www.istockphoto.com; Zorb Ltd, New Zealand.

Map designed by © Alison Davies at The Mapping Company Ltd 2007

This book is produced using paper that is made from wood grown in managed, sustainable forests. It is natural, renewable and recyclable. The logging and manufacturing processes conform to the environmental regulations of the country of origin.

Typeset by Palimpsest Book Production Ltd, Grangemouth, Stirlingshire
Printed and bound in King's Lynn, England by Biddles Ltd

ACKNOWLEDGEMENTS

No one's got time to sit down and read pages of acknowledgements when there are adventure sports out there to do, but on the basis that there are always a few blank pages at the beginning of a book to fill, briefly. . .

This book could only have been written with a lot of support, advice and tactful editing suggestions from the passionate people out there who live, breathe and eat the adventure sports written about in this book. Thank you to John Carr, Mark Gransbury, Liz Packer, Rob Barber, Roger Payne, Andy Coomes, Richard Gowers, Jem Howe, Gary Denton, Lee Bartlett, Rob Comber, Chris Wright, Matt Moore, Judy Leden, Colin Bodill, Robin Durie, Jon Warren, Ashley Charlwood, Fiona Pascoe, James Allison, Matt Ferris and the many other people we have spoken to along the way.

Robert Foss, Lucy Beevor and all the team at A & C Black; you were a brave lot to take us on when we came up with the idea for the book. Thank you, and we are looking forward to the next one.

Wendy Casterton, demon researcher, proofreader and stickler for accuracy; Irvine and I would still be floundering over the first few pages without you.

And finally for their patience, supper-making skills and endless support, big thanks to George Crawford and Sophia Kauntze.

CONTENTS

WATER

INTRODUCTION

Been sitting at your desk this week counting down the days until the weekend and wondering what to do when it arrives? Sick of the sight of your computer? Think there must be more to weekends than hangovers, reality TV shows and Sunday night blues? Crave some real excitement, exhilaration and going back to work on Monday morning still buzzing from your weekend? Then you're reading the right book.

Here at Ride of My Life we've thrown desks, paperclips and purchase orders to the wind so that we can make our passion for adventure sports yours.

This book, the UK's only guide to adventure sports, provides you with information about all the many thrilling sports on offer in the British Isles and where you can go to do them. This book is aimed at those of you who might be trying things for the first time and may just want a few great weekends of fun; but it's also for those who want to take a sport to the next level and participate in competitions, get a licence or even become an instructor.

At Ride of My Life we're not about *extreme* sports, we're about *adventure* sports. We all have different passions, we all have different fears – some of us love heights, others get giddy in high heels; some of us love water, others take baths with armbands on. But if you're reading this book, we all have one thing in common: adventure. We all want to live our lives more, have more fun and push ourselves a bit further. And that is why we have not only put together a great book (modesty is our middle name), but we have also come up with our unique Ride of My Life ratings.

So what are these unique ratings and how do they work? Well, we wanted to know which sports gave us the biggest 'Thrill Factor' and how to get the best 'Buzz for Your Buck', or in other words calculate how much of an adrenaline kick we could get for a first-time experience for each adventure sport. So we recorded our resting heart rate, and then recorded it again when we took part in each sport. We used these rates to determine a 'Thrill Factor' relative to each sport on a scale of 1–10. We then divided the 'Thrill Factor' with the cost per hour for a beginner to take part in the sport and this gave us our 'Buzz for Your Buck' rating. Hey presto, we have our unique Ride of My Life ratings.

Now, we should mention that results will vary for all of us as we all have different resting heart rates and all have various individual fears. And that is where you come in. We want some help from you, whether you are experienced or a novice, to refine and compare the ratings further. To contribute, log on to our website at www.rideofmylife.com and visit the ratings page to find out how you can record your results and compare your ratings with other adventure sport enthusiasts out there. With your help we can provide the definitive guide to what sports will give you the best 'Thrill Factor' and 'Buzz for your Buck'. We've also listed three sports as off the ratings: BASE jumping (because none of us are qualified or crazy enough to jump), Parkour and Free Running (because it takes many months of practice to reach a decent standard) and Adventure Racing, which is more of an endurance event.

Mondays at Elastic Heights – Ride of My Life's HQ – always start with recounting excitedly the adventure sports we have all been taking part in over the weekend; tales of daring, nerve-conquering moments, adrenaline highs or just sheer fun and pleasure. They always end with planning what we are going to do the following weekend. So quite simply, we are bringing you the *Guide to Adventure Sports: UK* so that your Monday mornings can be as great as ours.

But remember, don't sit around reading this book for too long – get out there and have the ride of your life.

Emma Drew and Irvine Conner

TOP 10 SPORTS BY 'BUZZ FOR YOUR BUCK'

Rank	Category	Sport
1	Land	Mountain boarding
2	Water	Kite surfing
3	Land	Mountain biking
4	Air	Bungee jumping
5	Water	Water skiing, wakeboarding, hydrofoiling
6	Land	Caving
7	Water	White water rafting
8	Water	Jet skiing
9	Land	Abseiling, freefall rappelling, rap jumping
10	Land	Kite landboarding, kite buggying, buggy jumping

TOP 10 SPORTS BY 'THRILL FACTOR'

Rank	Category	Sport
1	Air	Parachuting and freefalling
2	Air	Bungee jumping
3	Water	Kite surfing
4	Air	Flying jets and aerobatics
5	Air	Hang gliding
6	Water	White water rafting
7	Land	Karting
8	Air	Paragliding
9	Air	Microlighting
10	Water	Power boating

A FREE BACON ROLL?

There is no such thing as a free breakfast (although drop into Elastic Heights and we'll shout you a bowl of cornflakes). You can't just pay your money, read this book and go off and do the sports. Oh no. This is a two-way street and we want to hear from you. We want you to tell us all your tales of daring-do, see your photos, ogle your video clips and talk to you about how much fun you're having. So visit our website www.rideofmylife.com and you can upload all of this and share it with the millions of other people out there who are having as much fun as we all are.

(And you will even find some photos of the lycra-clad office gang at Elastic Heights on there . . . just make sure you are not eating your lunch when you take a look. We cannot be held responsible for the consequences or cleaning bills).

HOW TO USE THIS BOOK

Read it. That's pretty much it.

Oh, and for ease of use we have divided the book up into three sections: air, land and water. And our lovely publishers at A&C Black have really spoiled us and raided their piggy banks to provide a map, which shows you how the geography of the listings works for each sport (see page *xv*). So when you have read about a sport, we have then provided you with a list of clubs, societies and commercial companies where you can find out more or take part.

And while we are on the subject of clubs and societies, we are keen to promote the many brilliant ones that are all around the UK. You will find their members are hugely dedicated to their sport and have a wealth of first-hand knowledge and wisdom. Not all clubs and societies can teach beginners (often due to insurance and legal requirements), but many will be happy to talk to you and offer their recommendations of where you can go and do the sport as a beginner.

Importantly, we would also like to add that in listing these clubs, societies and commercial companies, we are neither recommending nor rating them. We are providing you with a starting point. There are many, many more excellent organisations out there and as you find out about them and use them, we would like you to tell us so that we can include them in the next editions of this book and on our website at www.rideofmylife.com

In the listings, we have included only the names of clubs and their websites. We haven't listed contact numbers because, for many clubs, they are contactable through the home and work telephone numbers of committee members. The committee of a club will often change, so rather than frustrate you with lists of numbers that may be incorrect by the time you go to use them, we have included just the websites. Individual websites will then give you the name and number of the current person you need to contact.

A WORD FROM AUNTIE EDNA. . .

Before you go off gallivanting and trying the sports written about in this book, do make sure you:

- call the centre or company you want to visit and book ahead
- ask them what, if any, equipment you need to take with you
- check whether they have any age, health, fitness or ability criteria that might prevent you from taking part in the sport
- make sure you use a reputable company – ask people for recommendations if you are unsure
- wear a vest in winter.

Elgin
Inverness
Aberdeen
Fort William
Scotland
Oban
Perth
Glasgow
Edinburgh
Dumfries
Londonderry
Northern Ireland
Belfast
Carlisle
Newcastle Upon Tyne
Penrith
Northern England
Scarborough
Harrogate
Lancaster
York
Leeds
Hull
Manchester
Sheffield
Lincoln
East Midlands
Denbigh
Nottingham
Grantham
Stoke-on-Trent
Derby
King's Lynn
Shrewsbury
Norwich
Leicester
Peterborough
Aberystwyth
Wales & West Midlands
Cambridge
Bury St Edmunds
Bedford
East of England
Ipswich
Banbury
Oxford
Cardiff
Swindon
Reading
LONDON
Bristol
Basingstoke
Maidstone
Barnstaple
Taunton
Salisbury
South-east
Folkestone
South-west
Southampton
Bournemouth
Brighton
Hastings
Plymouth
Penzance
NORTH
0
50 miles
0
100 kilometres

AIR

PAGE 12 BUNGEE JUMPING

AGE 27
ANG GLIDING

PAGE 48
PARAGLIDING

PAGE 21
GLIDING

PAGE 42 PARACHUTING AND FREEFALLING

PAGE 48
PARAGLIDING
PAGE 56
SCAD DIVIN
PAGE 17
FLYING JETS AND
AEROBATICS
PAGE 42
SKYDIVING

LAND

PAGE 118
ZORBING

PAGE 102
MOUNTAIN BIKING

PAGE 61
ABSEILING

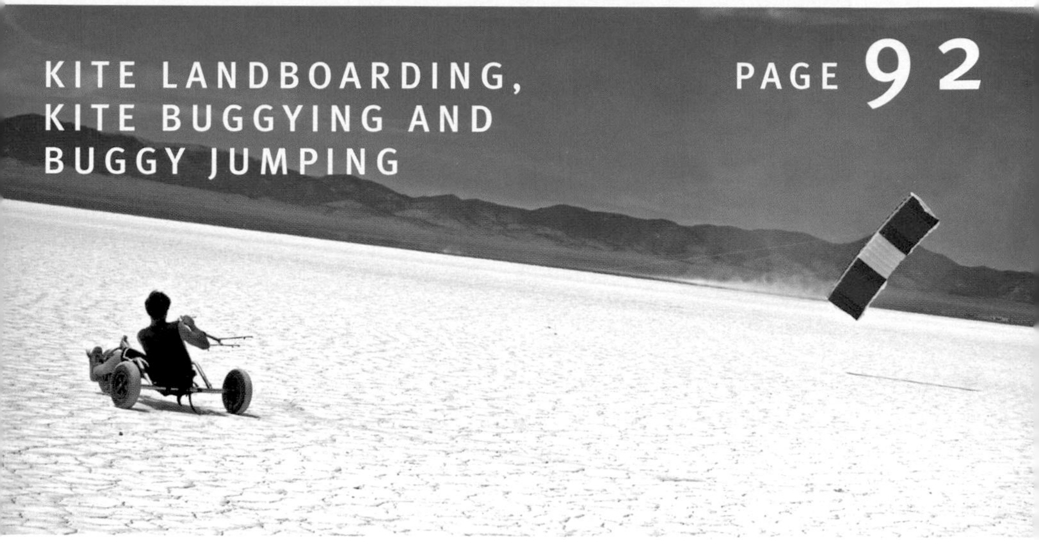
KITE LANDBOARDING, KITE BUGGYING AND BUGGY JUMPING
PAGE 92

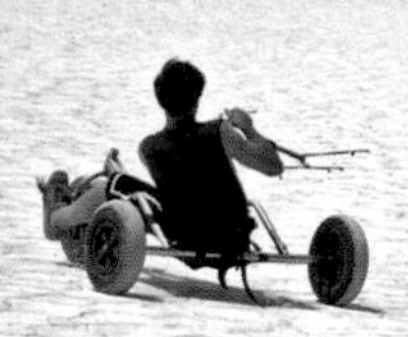

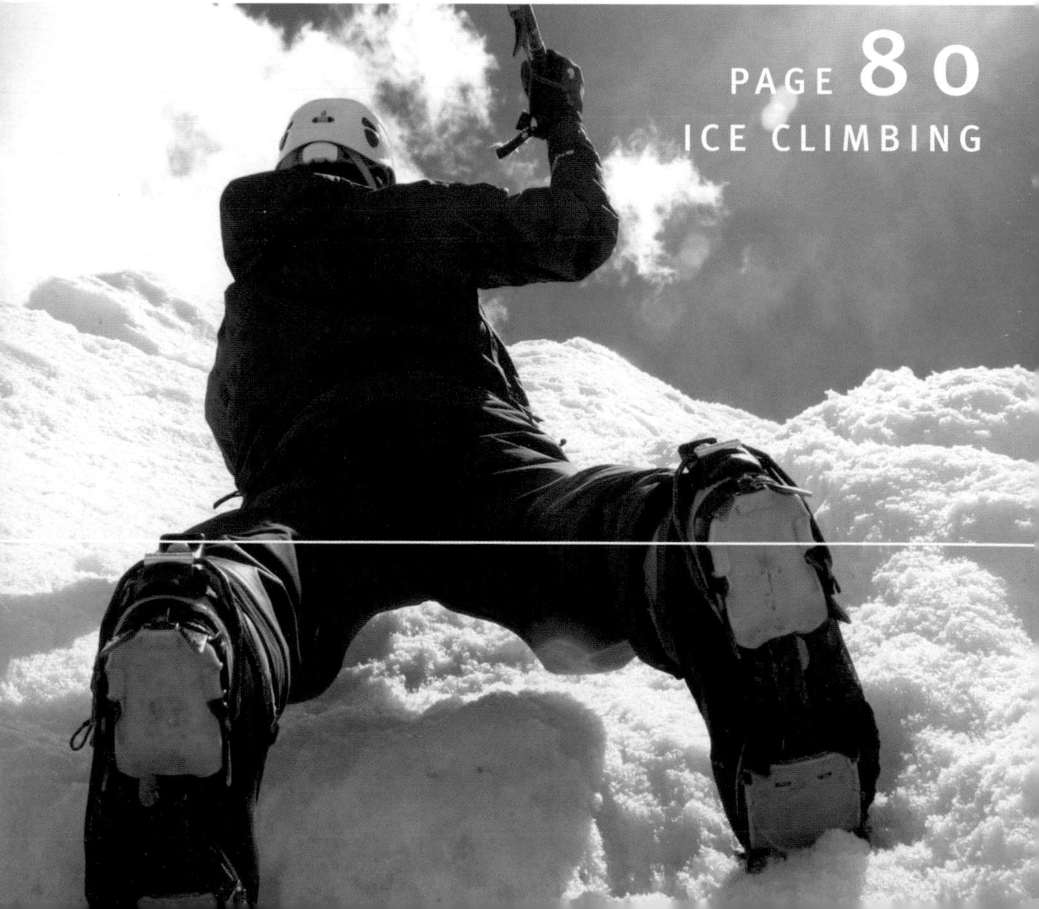
PAGE 80
ICE CLIMBING

PAGE 76
CAVING

PAGE 80
CLIMBING

PAGE 106
MOUNTAIN BOARDING

PAGE 113
QUAD BIKING

PAGE 66
ADVENTURE RACING

WATER

PAGE 182
WINDSURFING

PAGE 156 POWER BOATING

PAGE 167
SURFING

PAGE 123
BODYBOARDING

PAGE 172
HYDROFOILING

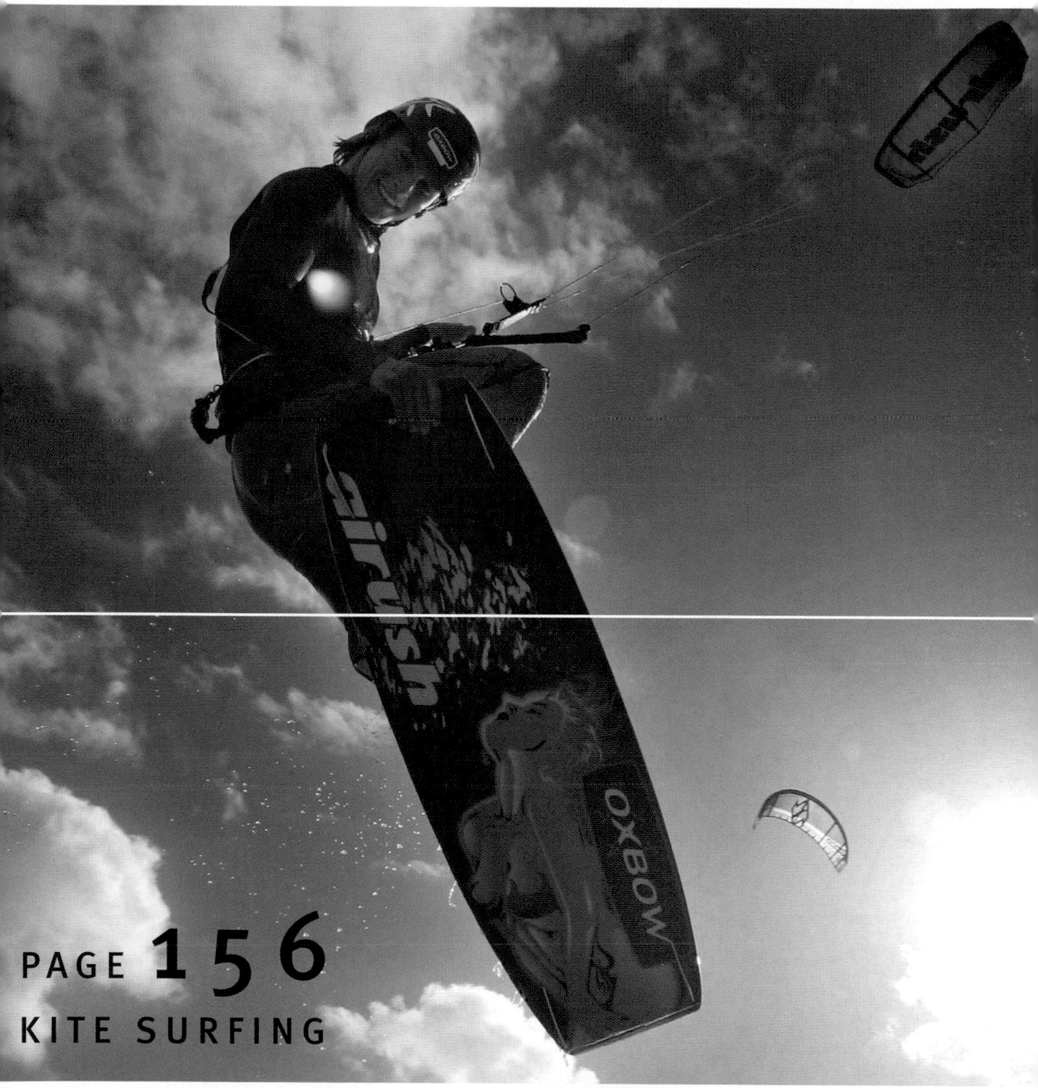

PAGE 156
KITE SURFING

PAGE 147
JET SKIING

PAGE 178
WHITE WATER RAFTING

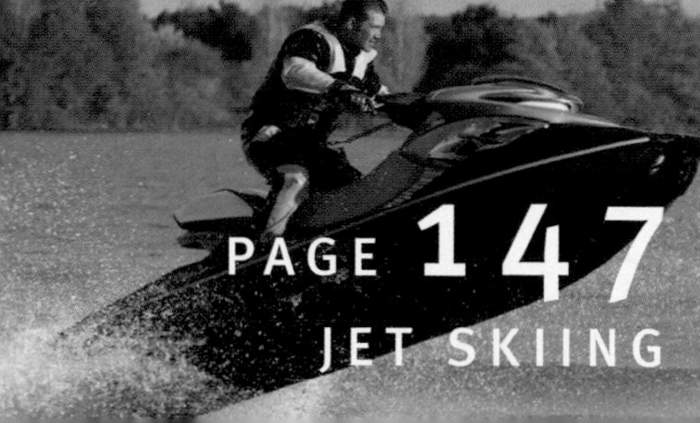

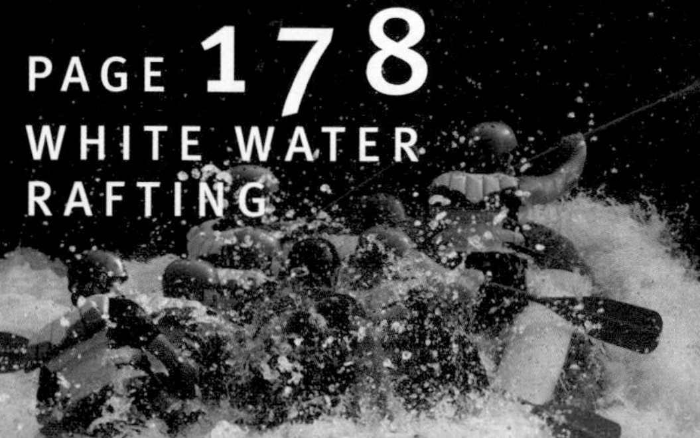

PAGE 172
WATER SKIING

AIR

TOP 5 AIR SPORTS BY 'BUZZ FOR YOUR BUCK'

Rank	Sport
1	Bungee jumping
2	Microlighting
3	Gliding
4	Hang gliding
5	Parachuting and freefalling

TOP 5 AIR SPORTS BY 'THRILL FACTOR'

Rank	Sport
1	Parachuting and freefalling
2	Bungee jumping
3	Flying jets and aerobatics
4	Hang gliding
5	Paragliding

01 BALLOONING

BUZZ FOR YOUR BUCK 1/10
THRILL FACTOR ■□□□□□□□□□

'What did the chicken say to the duck and the sheep? . . . Let's go hot air ballooning!'

On 19th September 1783, the Montgolfier brothers launched the first hot air balloon. Their intrepid passengers were a rooster, a duck and a sheep. The balloon stayed in the air for a grand total of 15 minutes before crashing down to earth. Over 200 years later, hot air ballooning is one of the most popular sports in the UK. Safety records are excellent – although it would seem chickens, ducks and sheep remain sceptical as they're rarely seen clambering into balloon baskets these days! In fact, hot air ballooning in the UK is probably the safest aerial sport. Statistics indicate that you are at greater risk when driving by car to the launch site than when hot air ballooning.

Ballooning's popularity in the UK abounds. There are few experiences as serene and peaceful as lifting up through the morning mist or early evening

BALLOONING . . . NOT JUST A LOAD OF HOT AIR

light and floating off to capture a bird's-eye view of the land below. If this aerial adventure isn't enough of a thrill, why not join the growing numbers of balloonists who compete in races or attempt to break speed and duration records? You could even go one better and enjoy ballooning over more unorthodox terrain such as the Alps or the Grand Canyon.

If you are looking to take part in adventure sports but want to ease yourself in gently, rather than throwing yourself out of a plane or scaling a sheer rock face on your first weekend, then ballooning is definitely for you. And for those who are keen adventure sports enthusiasts already, what better way to relax than to take a balloon ride and enjoy the euphoria of hanging peacefully in the silent stillness of the air?

GETTING INVOLVED

GETTING STARTED

Ballooning is a relatively easy sport to get involved in. Before becoming the next altitude or speed record challenger, you can try a taster day with one of the many companies that take people ballooning. If this is not a gift flight then remember to take a bottle of champagne to crack open when you return to *terra firma* – a tradition in the ballooning world. A one-off experience balloon flight will last around an hour. Companies and/or clubs offer different rates, so it is worth shopping around. You may get discounts for larger groups, so remember to ask.

There is no age restriction for ballooning but you must be able to climb in and out of the basket and stand for the duration of the flight. If you are in any doubt, consult your GP before booking. If you want to take children, make sure they are over 1.2 metres (4 feet) tall or you will need to provide a running commentary due to their inability to see over the side of the basket.

TAKING IT FURTHER

If you enjoyed your taster day and want to get more involved with ballooning, the first step is to join the British Balloon and Airship Club (BBAC) and a local club. The cost of membership for regional and local clubs varies; check the club's website for details. Both regional and local clubs can help you find pilots who need a crew. Once you have become a qualified balloon crew member, you can train for a range of licences for balloons (listed below). After that, the sky is – quite literally – the limit!

Getting your pilot's licence

As a registered aircraft, hot air balloons must comply to the same licensing requirements as any fixed wing aircraft or helicopter. There are several licences you can train for:

- to fly a balloon you will need a Pilot's Licence
- to fly yourself and friends you need a Private Pilot's Licence (PPL(B))
- to fly passengers or fly for a company, you need a Commercial Pilot's Licence (CPL(B)).

If you want to study for the PPL(B), you can do most of your training with any private pilot. You must complete at least 16 hours of hands-on flying experience within a rolling 24-month period, and at least four of these flights must be with a registered instructor. You will also need to sit written exams in Air Law, Meteorology, Navigation, Balloon Systems and Human Performance and Limitations, as well as attend a seminar on landowner relations.

When your training pilot considers you ready, you will take a Recommendation Flight with an instructor (a mock exam). If the instructor agrees that you're ready for Check-out, he will sign your Recommendation. The next step is a Check-out Flight with an examiner. If this is satisfactory, you can then make a Solo Flight and apply for your PPL(B).

Getting your PPL(B) isn't a cheap business, you can expect to pay £4500 to £6000, but there are ways you can save costs. Most sport balloon pilots don't pay crews in cash but are willing to give lessons in return, so this can be a cheaper way to learn.

Those interested in acquiring a Commercial Pilot's Licence (CPL(B)) should contact the BBAC (see opposite for details).

With the cost of a hot air balloon starting at around £25,000, joining a club and using their facilities to get started helps to make an expensive sport accessible to all.

WHERE TO GET INVOLVED

ADMINISTRATIVE BODIES

The British Balloon and Airship Club (BBAC)
www.bbac.org.uk
0117 953 1231
BBAC, St John's Street, Bedminster, Bristol BS3 4NH

The BBAC is a volunteer-based organisation which promotes the safety, enjoyment and advancement of lighter-than-air flight in all its forms – hot-air ballooning, gas ballooning and airships. The Club is active in looking after the interests of its members by representing them in discussions with official organisations including the Civil Aviation Authority (CAA) and the international air sports governing bodies such as the FAI and CIA.

CLUBS, SOCIETIES AND COMPANIES

South East & London

3-4-40 Region
www.3440.org

Black Horse Ballooning Club
www.bh-bc.co.uk

Chiltern Region British Balloon and Airship Club
www.crbbac.org

London Region Balloon Club
www.lrbc.ballooning.org.uk
020 8150 9282

Mid Hants Balloon Club
www.midhantsballoonclub.org.uk

South West

Western Region British Balloon and Airship Club (WRBBAC)
www.wrbbac.co.uk

East Midlands & East Anglia

East Midlands Balloon Group (EMBG)
www.embg.org.uk

Northern England

North West Balloon and Airship Club
www.nwbac.com
01282 603696

Pennine Region Balloon Association
www.prba.org.uk

Scotland

There are currently no ballooning clubs or societies in Scotland but the following commercial companies offer gift flights and some offer pilots' training.

Scotair Balloons
www.scotair.com
01899 860334

Alba Ballooning
www.albaballooning.co.uk
0131 667 4251

Northern Ireland

Sperrin Balloon Club
www.ballooning-in-ireland.com
0771 8651788

02 BASE JUMPING

OFF THE RATINGS!

BASE jumpers leap off fixed points and have just seconds to open a small parachute or face certain death. The acronym BASE stands for the four categories of objects from which people jump and freefall:

- **B**uilding
- **A**ntenna (an uninhabited tower such as an aerial mast)
- **S**pan (a bridge, arch or dome)
- **E**arth (a cliff or other natural formation).

Considered a fringe extreme sport, and beyond the most adventurous of adventure sports, the acronym BASE should really stand for Basically, About, Securing, Extinction.

BASE jumping is a relative newcomer to adventure sports. Its birth in 1980 is attributed to a Norwegian, Carl Boenish. In 1975, Boenish went to Yosemite National Park to film some hang gliding footage. A pivotal event in the history of BASE jumping, the hang gliding session concluded with two men flying down the middle of the valley, releasing themselves into freefall and parachuting into the valley below. Boenish was the first person to apply modern gear (ram air parachutes) and modern freefall techniques (tracking) to fixed object jumps.

Boenish was killed in 1984 jumping a cliff in Norway. By this time, the sport of fixed jumping had taken root and had been named BASE jumping (in 1981). The legend of Boenish, the father of modern BASE jumping, lives on today.

BASE jumping is not for those who are new to, or have even done most adventure sports. It is for extremely seasoned adventure sports enthusiasts who have the desire and motivation to put in serious amounts of training time (and money) in order to go to the next level of the adrenaline rush. We can't deny it will give you a thrill beyond measure (in fact, it's off the Ride of my Life ratings), but it's not something you should attempt on a stag weekend. BASE jumping is neither a hobby nor a pastime – it's a lifestyle: jumpers live, sleep and breathe BASE. And, although it might help your pulling power in the pub, most people will probably just think you're crazy for doing it. Arguably, some would say you *have* to be mad to BASE jump.

BASE JUMPERS COME FROM ALL OVER THE WORLD TO JUMP THE KJAERAG IN NORWAY

GETTING INVOLVED

BASE jumping is not for everyone. In fact, it's probably only for a very few people. If you are seriously thinking about doing it, you should evaluate yourself objectively and ask yourself a few questions:

- Are you conscious of everything around you at all times?
- When you knock over a bottle of beer, do you manage to right it before you've spilled most of it?
- How often do you trip or stumble?

BASE jumpers must have lightning-fast reactions.

GETTING STARTED

If you have answered the above questions and you still think you're right for BASE jumping, then you will need to have at least 200 skydives under your belt. Skydives are crucial to developing accuracy, tracking and canopy skills. You will also need to be comfortable with parachutes and freefall, and be able to make split-second decisions. BASE jumpers need experience of multiple skydiving disciplines and dealing with canopy malfunctions.

All the experience you need before you start BASE jumping means that you will have spent considerable amounts of cash perfecting your skydiving techniques and canopy control. In addition to money, you'll also need nerves of steel, lightning-quick reactions and commitment to a particular way of life.

TAKING IT FURTHER

Still think you want to BASE jump? Then find a mentor – someone who has done 200 or more BASE jumps, who you think will be a good teacher, and who you will get along with. You will be trusting this person with your life, so make your choice carefully.

EQUIPMENT NEEDED

The equipment list for BASE jumping is neither short nor cheap. When the sport was starting out in the 1970s and 1980s, BASE jumpers used the same equipment that they used to skydive with at the drop zone. Then jumpers gradually started to modify their skydiving gear to make it more appropriate to fixed object jumping. Today, you need to buy a brand new Velcro-closed BASE-specific rig from a major manufacturer and put a real BASE canopy in it. People may try to sell you converted skydiving gear (Raven, Cruiselite, Pegasus, etc.) but you should buy only purpose-built BASE gear. Some manufacturers even offer training in the use of their equipment, a big step forward for new BASE jumpers who previously had to rely on knowledge transferred from base jumper to base jumper.

WHERE TO GET INVOLVED

ADMINISTRATIVE BODIES AND COMPANIES

There are no official bodies for BASE jumping in the UK, although the sport is gradually gaining recognition.

Check out www.basejumping.co.uk or www.basejumper.org for further information.

03

BUNGEE JUMPING

BUZZ FOR YOUR BUCK 3/10
THRILL FACTOR

When you argue with your girlfriend or wife, you might expect it to cost you a pair of shoes, an expensive dinner or 48 painful hours of her sulking and you grovelling. You probably wouldn't expect it to end in the invention of an adventure sport that would be recognised and practised worldwide.

Well, that's just what happened in the village of Bunlap on the South Island of Pentecost, when a man called Tamalie rowed with his wife. Seemingly, she shunned his offer of new shoes and a meal out, taking instead the unexpected decision to climb a Banyan tree and wrap her ankles in liana vines. He followed her up the tree, but when he got too close, she threw herself off the edge. Not knowing what she'd done, he threw himself off too. He died, but she survived – and the sport of vine jumping was invented. The men of Bunlap were so impressed by her performance that they practised these jumps in case they ever found themselves in the same situation. To this day, the men of Pentecost jump off trees to prove their manhood (and presumably to avoid the costly business of buying post-row shoes).

3. . . 2. . . 1. . . BUNGEEEEEEEE!

Modern day bungee jumping started on 1st April 1979, when a group of people from the Oxford Dangerous Sport Club, impressed by a film about the 'vine jumpers', jumped from the 75-metre (245-feet) Clifton Suspension Bridge in Bristol. Using nylon-braided rubber shock cord instead of vines, and dressed in top hat and tails, they performed a four-man simultaneous jump. The enthusiasts were promptly arrested, but bungee jumping hit the world press the next day.

Bungee jumping is probably one of the easiest adventure sports to get started with as there is virtually no training required. You simply turn up at a bungee site and jump. But be warned – after each jump, you'll want to find a higher jump to aim for, so it's advisable not to make your first jump the world's highest (found in South Africa, a staggering 216 metres/708 feet).

There are also several alternatives to the standard bungee jump:

- Reverse bungee, sometimes called Catapult, involves you being anchored to the ground while the cord is stretched upwards. Once fully extended, the anchor holding you in place is released and you rush skywards.
- Sitting in a cage (sometimes in tandem) while two cords are stretched upwards on two towers. The cage is anchored and released when ready.

Bungee jumping is ideal for those who have limited time for adventure sports – perhaps just a few hours – and who want an incredible adrenaline rush and great buzz for their money. You won't want to keep going back and doing the same jump time and time again, but there are many different bungee jump sites across the UK.

GETTING INVOLVED

Some operators have a minimum age limit of 14 years, and some ask that jumpers over 50 years of age provide a medical certificate signed by their doctor. You will not be permitted to jump if you are pregnant, have high blood pressure, heart problems, epilepsy or asthma. Call bungee sites ahead of your visit, so you can check the restrictions in advance.

Prices start from £40, with extra fees if you want the T-shirt, video etc.

GETTING STARTED

Once you have booked your jump and arrived at the jump site, training typically consists of an explanation of the procedure. You'll be weighed by a trained operator and the length of the bungee jump will be adjusted accordingly. Padded ankle straps will be fastened securely before you step on to the bridge platform or crane. If on a crane, you and the operator will be hoisted up (and up), and when the crane stops you will turn to face outwards. There's only one thing to do now – jump! There is usually a countdown of *3, 2, 1, Bungee!* Don't even think about hesitating at this point – think of the video and the people watching. It's also much harder to leave the platform after a false start.

There are many travelling bungee jump experiences, but some of the best are static cranes because they are often higher. Remember, the higher the crane, the longer you fall and the bigger the thrill. Check out www.ukbungee.co.uk for a full list of locations and dates.

TAKING IT FURTHER

For those of you who want to combine the adrenaline rush of an aerial sport with the thrills of a water sport, then some bungee jump sites have the facility to jump over water. Here, you'll fall past ground level where the crane is standing and enter the water head first – perhaps as deep as your waist – before being thrown back up into the air as the elastic recoils. You'll be left dripping wet and experiencing an unforgettable adrenaline high.

EQUIPMENT NEEDED

As the jumper, the only equipment you'll need is a strong stomach and nerves. Just turn up to the bungee clothed (although some choose to omit this part!) and everything else will be provided. Some commercial operators use a simple ankle attachment while others use a body harness, if only as backup for an ankle attachment. And it may not be your job to do so, but it's always worth checking that the cord is attached before you jump.

WHERE TO GET INVOLVED

ADMINISTRATIVE BODIES

British Elastic Rope Sports Association (BERSA)
www.bungeezone.com/orgs/bersa.shtml
01865 311179
33a Canal Street, Oxford OX2 6BQ

The British Elastic Rope Sports Association (BERSA) exists to promote safety by regulation of the sport in the UK. BERSA is responsible for ensuring the highest standards of safety are maintained at certified clubs, and for training and licensing their staff. Furthermore, because BERSA is a non-profit-making body, it is able to act as a centre of expertise, encouraging an on-going programme of research and development of the sport.

COMPANIES

Bungee jumping tends to be carried out by commercial organisations, rather than clubs and societies.

The UK Bungee Club
www.ukbungee.co.uk
07000 286 433
Rockwood Cottages, 43 Barnsley Road, Flockton, Wakefield WF4 4DW

A commercial organisation, the UK Bungee Club is the largest bungee club in the UK, with jump locations across the country. The club was established in 1992 and has safely jumped over 100,000 people. Specialising in mobile events, the club has the world's only indoor operation, based in Sheffield. Check out the website (www.ukbungee.co.uk) for dates and locations. Pre-booking is essential.

04

FLYING JETS AND AEROBATICS

BUZZ FOR YOUR BUCK 1/10
THRILL FACTOR ■■■■■■□□□□

FLYING JETS

If there is any job that is going to make you utterly irresistible to the opposite sex, it's got to be that of a fighter pilot. Step into a MiG-25 and fly at Mach 2.5 on the edge of space, and you'll instantly become a sex god or goddess. Loudly recount your tales of flying 1 mile every 2 seconds, diving from 1220 metres (4000 feet) to 30 metres (100 feet) and clipping air socks as you fly by control towers, and you'll have the best looking people in town begging you for a date. So, if you're having sleepless nights worrying about how to spend your annual bonus or lottery win, worry no more. A flight in a fighter jet is a truly awesome, adrenaline-fuelled experience that will be very hard to top. Save up the money and treat yourself to this unforgettable experience.

GETTING INVOLVED

Move over Maverick, Ice Man and Goose – bold, daring readers (with larger than average bank balances and no overdraft) are getting into the cockpit.

Do this and you'll be joining the very few people who have seen the earth from the breathtaking vista of 25 kilometres (82,000 feet) and have witnessed the view overhead as the sky fades into the darkness of space. From the cockpit you'll see the curvature of the earth – an 1100-kilometre (685-mile) horizon – but hold on tight as the pilot demonstrates high-speed air manoeuvres. Tail slides, barrel rolls, high-g turns and dives are guaranteed to take you to a new level of thrill seeking.

GETTING STARTED

To buy your own MiG-25 will set you back millions of pounds, and the second-hand or 'nearly new' market in the UK these days is somewhat limited. A one-off trip (based in Russia) with a pilot will set you back around £15,000 for a top-of-the-range flight in a MiG-25. Subsequent pulling power and kudos? Priceless.

AEROBATICS: A TRULY UNFORGETTABLE EXPERIENCE

EQUIPMENT NEEDED

A deep pocket, a strong stomach and (possibly) a sick bag.

AEROBATICS

If flying jets will make too large a dent in your bank balance, then why not take to the skies for a thrilling half-hour of aerobatics flying?

Many commercial organisations offer trial flying lessons and aerobatics experiences in aircraft such as the de Havilland Chipmunk, Slingsby Firefly and CAP10. These aircraft are capable of extreme manoeuvres, so going up for a flight with a qualified pilot will see you loop-the-loop, fly upside down, swoop low, twist, and swoop high again. . . Hold on to your stomach and nerves – this will be the experience of a lifetime.

All aerobatics flights are flown as a trial flying lesson with a Civil Aviation Authority (CAA) qualified flying instructor, who will give you the opportunity to take control. It is all very 'Hollywood', but without the big budget.

GETTING INVOLVED

As long as you're fit and agile enough to climb in and out of the cockpit, then you should be able to take part in aerobatics flying. It is not advisable to participate if you are pregnant. Some companies have height and weight restrictions, so check beforehand. If you suffer from epilepsy, fits, recurrent fainting, giddiness or blackouts, high blood pressure or heart conditions, you should check with the centre you're flying from before booking a flight.

Prices vary depending on how long you want to play in the clouds. Expect to pay between £100 and £150 for a 20-minute flight, and be prepared to be the envy of all your friends.

EQUIPMENT NEEDED

You don't need any equipment for aerobatics flying apart from soft-soled shoes. You will be supplied with a flying jacket and helmet if you're going up in an open-cockpit aircraft, and you will be given a headset to use.

WHERE TO GET INVOLVED

ADMINISTRATIVE BODIES

Civil Aviation Authority
www.caa.co.uk
020 7379 7311
CAA House, 45–59 Kingsway,
London WC2B 6TE

The Civil Aviation Authority (CAA) was established by an Act of Parliament in 1972 as an independent specialist aviation regulator and provider of air traffic services.

COMPANIES

There are many companies around the UK that will offer aerobatic experiences; an example is given below.

Experience Mad
www.experiencemad.co.uk
0870 7607432
Grand Adventures Ltd,
ICS House,
Hall Road,
Heybridge, Maldon,
Essex CM9 4LA

05

GLIDING

BUZZ FOR YOUR BUCK 2/10
THRILL FACTOR ■■■■□□□□□□

'Once you have tasted flight, you will walk the earth with your eyes turned forever skyward, for there you have been, and there you long to return.'

Leonardo Da Vinci *(1452–1519)*

For many people, gliding is the ultimate free-flying experience. Get up in the air and experience the same currents that birds use to fly, but do so in a piece of extraordinary engineering that allows you to reach top speeds of 275 km/h (170 mph). After you have covered up to 965 km (600 miles) in one day, at heights of up to 12 km (40,000 feet), we'll be astounded if the experience doesn't change your life forever.

For your gliding experience, you'll need to be launched into the air. This is usually done using one of two methods: aero-towing or winch-launching

GLIDING: SILENCE IS GOLDEN

(although the less common bungee launch and auto-tow may be used in some places).

- Aero-towing is when a light aircraft pulls the glider into the air using a strong tow-rope. The glider will be towed to 450 or 600 metres (1500 or 2000 feet). When you reach the desired height, the tow-rope is released.
- For winch-launching, the glider is attached to a steel wire or synthetic-fibre cable, some 1000–1600 metres (3300–5250 feet) in length. This is pulled in using a stationary ground-based winch mounted on a heavy vehicle, which propels the glider into the air. The cable is released at a height of 400–500 metres (1300–1600 feet), after a short and steep ride. Using this launch method, you'll typically reach a height of around 300 metres (1000 feet) but, with the right conditions, heights of 600 metres (2000 feet) can be achieved.

Once launched, you'll experience the awe-inspiring silence of gliding through the air without an engine.

Your first flights will be in a dual-controlled glider with an instructor. When you've 50 or more supervised flights under your belt, you'll be ready to fly solo.

Your first solo flight will earn you an 'A badge', but we think the buzz you'll get from this beautiful sport will tempt you into going for your 'Silver C badge', awarded to pilots gaining an altitude of at least 1000 metres (3300 feet) and who have completed a five-hour flight and a cross-country flight of 50 km (31 miles). Then there's the 'Gold' and 'Diamond' badges for higher and longer flights. You can also fly competitively – some races have up to 50 gliders taking to the air at one time.

Aerobatics is an increasingly popular form of gliding for experienced pilots who are looking for increased challenge and thrill. Aerobatics displays and competition flying typically involve pilots performing routines at a starting height of 1.2 km (4000 feet) and at speeds of around 200 k/ph (130 mph). Contact the British Aerobatics Association via their website at www.aerobatics.org.uk for more information on this amazing sport.

The sport of gliding is accessible to everyone: from those who want to experience an hour-long taster session or one-day course, to those who want to dedicate more time to the sport, get a gliding badge, and perhaps join a syndicate and share ownership of a glider.

GETTING INVOLVED

Gliding is a sport that can be enjoyed at all levels, from the thriving club scene and aerobatics to the international racing competitions currently dominated by UK pilots. Today, the UK boasts five gliding World champions – could you be the next? There's also no age limit for gliding. You can fly solo on your 16th birthday and you can keep on flying for as long as you can sit in the cockpit. However, the limitations of glider design mean that people weighing over 102 kg (16 stone) or taller than 1.9 metres (6 feet 3 inches) cannot normally take part, but do check with the company.

GETTING STARTED

A trial flight and lesson is available from most clubs and is a great way to start your interest in gliding. The price of a trial flight starts at around £65. Vouchers can be bought from the British Gliding Association (see contact details on page 25) and redeemed at any affiliated club.

TAKING IT FURTHER

If you want to fly solo – and that's what it's all about, after all – then it's worth shopping around as there are many good deals out there. Various clubs offer an inclusive fee to take you from beginner to solo flyer, and a weekly or fortnightly course is a great way to advance quickly. Prices start at around £500, but there are varying periods by which you should complete your first solo flight, so do look at the terms and conditions.

EQUIPMENT NEEDED

Gliders have surprisingly small cockpits and huge wingspans, and come in many shapes and sizes. Prices range from a few hundred pounds for a basic single-seat glider to £100,000 for a top of the range racing glider. Fortunately, you don't need to buy your own glider – clubs will generally provide two-seater gliders for instructional purposes, and most have single-seat gliders for those who are ready to fly solo. If you do manage to get hooked on gliding – and there is a real risk of this – you can keep costs down by joining a syndicate and sharing the maintenance costs.

The only other thing you might need is a good head for heights, but don't let any fear of heights stop you from trying this truly exhilarating experience. So go on, grab your sense of adventure and remember to accept that once up there, you'll probably never want to come down.

WHERE TO GET INVOLVED

ADMINISTRATIVE BODIES

British Gliding Association
www.gliding.co.uk
0116 253 1051
British Gliding Association,
Kimberley House, Vaughan Way,
Leicester LW1 4SE

The British Gliding Association is the governing body for 95 member clubs around the UK. It exists to regulate and promote gliding in Britain, and conducts annual safety reviews. For a full listing of the 95 clubs and to the find the one nearest to you, visit: www.gliding.co.uk/findaclub/ukmap.htm.

CLUBS AND SOCIETIES

South-east and London

East Sussex Gliding Club
www.sussexgliding.co.uk
01825 840764
Kitson Field, The Broyle, Ringmer, East Sussex BN8 5AP

Oxford Gliding Club
www.oxford-gliding-club.co.uk
01869 343265
RAF Weston on the Green, Nr Bicester, Oxon OX25 3TQ

Surrey Hills Gliding Club
www.southlondongliding.co.uk
0208 763 0091
Kenley Airfield, Kenley, Surrey
CR8 5YG

South-west

Bristol and Gloucestershire Gliding Club
www.bggc.co.uk
01453 860342
Nympsfield, Stonehouse,
Gloucestershire GL10 3TX

Devon and Somerset Gliding Club
www.dsgc.co.uk
01404 841386
North Hill Airfield, Broadhembury,
Honiton, Devon EX14 3LP

Dorset Gliding Club
www.dorsetglidingclub.freeserve.co.uk
01929 405599 (weekends)
Eyres Field, Puddletown Road,
Wareham, Dorset BH20 7NG

Shalbourne Soaring Society
www.shalbournegliding.co.uk
01264 731204
Rivar Hill Airfield, Henley,
Marlborough, Wiltshire SN8 3RJ

The Vale of White Horse Gliding Club
www.swindongliding.co.uk
01367 252706
Sandhill Farm Airfield, Shrivenham,
Swindon, Wiltshire

Wales and West Midlands

Black Mountains Gliding Club
www.talgarthgc.co.uk
01874 711463
The Airfield, Talgarth, Brecon, LD3 0EJ

WHERE TO GET INVOLVED

Staffordshire Gliding Club
www.staffordshiregliding.co.uk
01785 282575
Seighford Airfield, Seighford, Stafford, Staffordshire ST18 9QE

East Midlands

Lincolnshire Gliding Club
www.lincsglidingclub.co.uk
01507 607922
Strubby Airfield, Alford, Lincolnshire

The Soaring Centre
www.thesoaringcentre.co.uk
01858 880521
Husbands Bosworth Airfield, Husbands Bosworth, Lutterworth, Leicestershire LE17 6JJ

East of England

Essex Gliding Club
www.essexgliding.com
01992 522222

Norfolk Gliding Club
www.ngcglide.freeserve.co.uk
01379 677207
Tibenham Airfield, Norfolk NR16 1NT

Northern England

Borders Gliding Club
www.bordersgliding.co.uk
01668 216 284
Milfield Airfield, Northumberland

Northumbria Gliding Club
www.northumbria-gliding-club.co.uk
01207 561286
The Club House, Currock Hill, Chopwell, Newcastle Upon Tyne NE17 7AX

York Gliding Centre
www.yorkglidingcentre.co.uk
01904 738694
Rufforth Airfield, Rufforth, York YO23 3QA

Scotland

Cairngorm Gliding Club
www.gliding.org
01540 651317 (weekends only)
Feshie Airstrip, Feshiebridge, Kingussie, Inverness-shire PH21 1NG

Highland Gliding Club
www.highglide.co.uk
01343 860272 / 07790 761277
Easterton Airfield, Birnie, Nr Elgin, Moray, Scotland

Scottish Gliding Centre
www.scottishglidingcentre.co.uk
01592 840543
Portmoak Airfield, Scotlandwell, Nr Kinross, Scotland KY13 9JJ

Northern Ireland

Ulster Gliding Club
www.gliding.utvinternet.com
028 7775 0301 (weekends only)/ 07709 808276
Bellarena Airfield, Seacoast Road, County Londonderry

06 HANG GLIDING

BUZZ FOR YOUR BUCK 3/10
THRILL FACTOR

'Hang gliding is like no other feeling on earth. After 28 years of flying, every time I take to the skies it is still exhilarating. When a bird comes to join you in a thermal, flying wingtip to wingtip so you can see every feather on its wings and every fleck in its eyeball, it is a truly life-changing experience. Don't just read this book, come and join the rest of us and learn to fly like a bird!'

***Judy Leden MBE**, 3-times Women's World Champion, multiple World record holder and 6-times British Women's Champion*

AVOID THE TRAFFIC JAMS WITH HANG GLIDING

Hang gliding uses a simple craft made of a metal-framed fabric wing, which sounds as if it could have been created on Blue Peter using coat hangers and tissue paper (provided an adult is in the room when scissors are needed). In fact, a hang glider is a sophisticated machine built of aluminium and high-tech sail fabrics. The pilot hangs in a harness suspended from the frame, holding something very similar to bicycle handlebars, and controls the glider by shifting his or her body weight. Experience hang gliding and you'll get far more than your Blue Peter badge. You'll get the freedom of a bird, the thrill of your life and the envy of every motorist watching you from a traffic jam.

A hang glider can be launched into the air using several methods:

- from a hill as you face into the prevailing wind
- towed by a micro-light aircraft
- launched by a ground winch.

It's also possible to launch yourself from a flat field by adding a power unit to the hang glider (contained inside the harness). This process is rather cumbersomely named 'foot-launched-powered hang gliding'.

The sport is controlled by the Civil Aviation Authority and is self-regulated by the British Hang Gliding and Paragliding Association (BHPA). To become a hang glider pilot you'll need to train at a licensed school; a full training course will set you back about £1000. Once you've completed your training, you can join one of the many clubs around the country and take part in their activities. Most clubs will be only too happy for you to join them at their meetings before you obtain your licence, which is an excellent way of gaining invaluable guidance and help from experts.

There are also taster days you can do before deciding to undertake the full training. But if you're hoping a taster day will be enough, watch out and hold on tight to your wallet – hang gliding is addictive! Before you know where you are, you'll be setting yourself the challenge of competing in the thriving national and international scene. Who knows, one day you may even beat the UK distance record, which currently stands at 257 km (160 miles) and an altitude of 4.9 km (16,000 feet).

GETTING INVOLVED

Pilots fly from hill and tow sites controlled by the numerous BHPA clubs dotted around the country. The emphasis is on hill flying, but tow operations and aerotow facilities are available in lowland locations. Competitions are held at club, national and international level, and the UK often leads the way in World competitions.

GETTING STARTED

In contrast to paragliding, hang gliding is a technically more difficult sport, but the machine is capable of much higher speeds, better gliding performance and can be flown in stronger winds. The glider and all its related equipment are highly specialised (although easy to transport on your roof rack), but don't let this put you off. Hang gliding is the closest you'll get to flying like a bird, so to get started book yourself on a one-day taster course for around £140 and find out if this really is for you. Prepare to be hooked!

TAKING IT FURTHER

For a five-day Hang Gliding Elementary Course (EPC) you can expect to pay around £600. Once you have gained your EPC, you can then progress to a four-day Hang Gliding Club Pilot course, which costs around £500. If you already have a CPC for paragliding, then you can do a course to convert to hang gliding.

There are nearly 100 clubs affiliated to the British Gliding Association. Ask club members for advice on which of the schools offer a full training syllabus. Once you are qualified and really know what you're doing, you can fly in spectacular places such as the Alps or Pyrenees, where it is much easier to fly higher and further.

EQUIPMENT NEEDED

During training, you'll start on a third-generation hang glider, which is slow and forgiving and has a top speed of 48 km/h (30 mph). If you want to progress to club pilot level, you'll need to master fourth- and fifth-generation gliders, with top speeds of up to 97 km/h (60 mph). These require more skill in flight and, more importantly, a sound, well-practised landing technique.

Hang glider manufacturers, both in the UK and overseas, build machines that are respected the world over. A top-of-the range competition hang glider can cost over £4500 new, although sports machines with only slightly less performance cost between £2000 and £3500; second-hand hang gliders cost much less.

As a pilot, you'll need:

- a hang gliding helmet that leaves your ears free to hear the vital sounds of the airflow around you
- a flying suit (although practical, this isn't essential when you start)
- boots
- an emergency parachute (gliders won't fail in the air, but a mid-air collision is always a remote possibility)
- the all-important harness. You'll probably start by using a harness that allows your legs to dangle free, but will move on to a pod-type harness that encloses the whole length of the body and provides comfort, warmth and streamlining (and also makes you look alarmingly like a flying caterpillar).

WHERE TO GET INVOLVED

ADMINISTRATIVE BODIES

The British Hang Gliding and Paragliding Association (BHPA)
www.bhpa.co.uk
0116 261 1322
The Old School Room, Loughborough Road, Leicester LE4 5PJ

The BHPA covers hang gliding, paragliding, parascending and paramotoring, and has over 9000 members across the country.

The Scottish Hang Gliding and Paragliding Federation
www.flyingscot.f9.co.uk
01355 246 252

Regional clubs and schools
There are many BHPA-registered clubs around the country. We've listed just some of them here, but you'll find a full listing on the BHPA website at: www.bhpa.co.uk/bhpa/clubs/index.php. These clubs look after flying sites and offer guidance and coaching assistance for club pilots to advance to pilot certification (as required to fly cross country). They do not provide basic training.

If you are a beginner and want to access training or a trial flight, you should contact one of the BHPA-registered schools or call up your nearest club and ask them to recommend a school.

We've listed some of these schools below, but a full listing is found at: www.bhpa.co.uk/bhpa/schools/index.php.

South-east and London
CLUBS:
Dunstable Hang Gliding and Paragliding
www.dhpc.info
0208 367 8068

Sky Surfing Club
www.skysurfingclub.co.uk
(Petersfield area of Hampshire and West Sussex)

The Southern Hang Gliding Club
www.shgc.org.uk
info@shgc.org.uk
1 Stamford Cottages, Ripe Lane, Firle, East Sussex

SCHOOLS:
Green Dragons Airsports Academy
www.greendragons.co.uk
01883 652666
Warren Barn Farm, Slines Oak Road, Woldingham, Surrey CR3 7HN

South Downs Hang Gliding
www.southdownshanggliding.co.uk
07890 362648
Gibraltar Farm, Firle, East Sussex BN8 6NB

WHERE TO GET INVOLVED

South-west

CLUBS:

Avon Hang Gliding and Paragliding Club
www.avonhgpg.co.uk
E-mail: membership@avonhgpg.co.uk

Devon and Somerset Condors
www.dscondors.co.uk
01392 204253

Kernow Hang Gliding and Paragliding Association (Cornwall)
www.khpa.co.uk
01872 273839

Thames Valley Hang Gliding and Paragliding Club (Wiltshire)
www.tvhgc.co.uk
01344 872266
E-mail: membership@tvhgc.co.uk

Wessex Hang Gliding and Paragliding Club
www.wessexhgpg.org.uk
01202 311574
E-mail: secretary@wessexhgpc.org.uk

SCHOOLS:

Flight Culture
www.flightculture.co.uk
07833 107902
15 High Street, Fordington,
Dorchester, Dorset DT1 1JZ

Wales and West Midlands

CLUBS:

Long Mynd Soaring Club (Shropshire and East Wales)
www.longmynd.org
E-mail: membership@longmynd.org

Malvern Hang Gliding Club
www.malvern-hang.org.uk
07773 493 622

North Wales Hang Gliding and Paragliding Club
www.nwhgpc.org.uk

The South-east Wales Hang Gliding and Paragliding Club
www.sewhgpgc.co.uk
01656 648246

SCHOOLS:

Welsh Hang Gliding and Paragliding Centre
www.welshairsports.com
01873 854090 / 0791 4026004
Welsh Airsports, Wilberton House,
Frogmore Street,
Abergavenny NP7 5AL

East Midlands

CLUBS:

Derbyshire Soaring Club
www.derbyshiresoaringclub.org.uk
0709 2017770

WHERE TO GET INVOLVED

Midland Aerotow Group (Leicestershire)
(Jointly owned by Leicestershire Microlight Aircraft Club and the Mercian Hang Gliding Club)
www.lmac.org.uk

SCHOOLS:
Airways Airsports
www.airways-airsports.com
01335 344308
Darley Moor Airfield, Ashbourne, Derbyshire DE6 2ET
E-mail: office@airways-airsports.com

Derbyshire Flying Centre
www.d-f-c.co.uk
0845 108 1577

East of England
CLUBS:
Norfolk Hang Gliding and Paragliding Club
www.flynorfolk.co.uk

Suffolk Coastal Floaters Hang Gliding Club
www.scfhgc.org

Northern England
CLUBS:
Dales Hang Gliding and Paragliding Club
www.dhpc.org.uk
07720 425146
E-mail: contacts@dhpc.org.uk

Northumbria Hang Gliding and Paragliding Club
www.nhpc.org.uk
0191 523 6886 / 01661 842166

Pennine Soaring Club
www.penninesoaringclub.org.uk
E-mail:
secretary@penninesoaringclub.org.uk

SCHOOLS:
Pennine Flying School
www.pennineflyingschool.com
077920 79855
E-mail: info@pennineflyingschool.com

Scotland
CLUBS:
Aberdeen Hang Gliding and Paragliding Club
www.ahpc.org.uk
01224 326095

Lanarkshire and Lothian Soaring Club
www.llsclub.org.uk
E-mail: info@llsclub.org.uk

Northern Ireland
CLUBS:
The Ulster Hang Gliding and Paragliding Club
www.uhpc.f9.co.uk
028 3834 1544 / 07729 549163
E-mail: secretary@uhpc.f9.co.uk

SCHOOLS:
Aerosports
www.aerosports.co.uk
02893 341414 / 07879 632111
E-mail: ken@aerosports.co.uk

07

MICROLIGHTING

BUZZ FOR YOUR BUCK 3/10
THRILL FACTOR

'Becoming microlighting World Champion was an unforgettable moment. But then again so is every trip I take in a microlight. Nearly anyone can microlight, and nearly everyone should.'

***Colin Bodill**, former World Microlight Champion and holder of the World Record for flying a microlight solo around the world in 2000*

Microlighting enables you to enjoy the freedom of the skies. You fly by the seat of your pants, like a paraglider (see pages 48–55), but with an engine to get you up there in the first place. It's a bit like flying a motorbike. If that isn't enough to persuade you to have a go, then nothing is.

MILE'S HILTON-BARBER AND HIS CO-PILOT STEVE SMITH FLY THEIR MICROLIGHT OVER NORTH LANARKSHIRE

Microlights are small two-seater aircraft which come in two styles:

- a flex-wing microlight combines an open-air hang glider wing with a trike, wheels and engine.
- a fixed-wing microlight is more like a conventional aircraft.

You can fly a microlight just about anywhere, landing in small fields or other suitable areas. Why not make a really stylish entrance and turn heads by arriving at a party in your microlight? (Be sure to check that the garden is big enough first.)

Rather than having to run from a hilltop to launch, the microlight takes off from the ground with the aid of a rear-mounted engine and three-wheeled trike base, known as the pod. Instead of lying down under the wing to fly it, you park yourself comfortably in a sitting position. If you are flying with someone else, he or she will be sitting either in front of or behind you.

You fly a microlight just like a hang glider, turning the aircraft to the left or right by shifting your body weight; shift your body to the left and the microlight turns left. How simple is that? The brilliant thing about microlighting is that it's easy to learn and easy to do. Typically, you can expect to be flying solo after only 10–20 hours of tuition.

With microlights becoming easier and cheaper to fly, and none of the expensive and time-consuming training required to fly a light aircraft, it's a great sport for people with limited spare time and for whom the buzz of a small engine doesn't compromise their experience of near-free flight. Once hooked, you can set your sights high and aim to beat UK microlight pilot Colin Bodill's World Record for flying around the world solo. You'll just need to butter up your boss to let you have 99 days holiday to fly the 46,855 km (25,300 nautical miles).

GETTING INVOLVED

GETTING STARTED

The best way to get started is a day's taster course. If this makes your pants ping with excitement, then your next step would be to book yourself on to a week's course. This will entail about 5 hours of flying time and considerable time spent learning about microlights.

TAKING IT FURTHER

To get your microlight pilot licence, you'll need to pass five written exams, in Airlaw, Navigation, Meteorology, Human Performance and Limitations (HPL) and Theory of Flight. You'll also need to have clocked up a minimum of 25 hours of flying time, of which 10 hours of this must be solo flights, and have made two cross-country qualifying flights of 74 km (40 nautical miles) each.

Passing the General Flying Test (GFT) will qualify you to fly with a passenger. The GFT involves a short resume of the syllabus, which allows an examiner to ensure you have no holes in your knowledge of flying.

High standards in the sport are maintained by strict regulations laid down by the British Microlight Aircraft Association (BMAA), who are accountable to the Civil Aviation Authority (CAA).

Microlighting is accessible to the majority of people, but there is a maximum weight limit, which varies from between 89–102 kg (14 and 16 stone). You'll also need to be aged over sixteen to fly (although at some locations, fourteen is the minimum age limit). Pilots aged under eighteen normally need to be accompanied to the venue by an adult and have a disclaimer form signed by a parent or guardian. The other thing to bear in mind is that flying solo requires constant decision making. Good planning skills and common sense are essential when dealing with the vagaries and potential dangers of the British weather.

BRIAN MILTON AND KEITH REYNOLDS ON THEIR 'ROUND THE WORLD IN 80 DAYS' TRIP IN 1998

EQUIPMENT NEEDED

For taster sessions and short courses, the schools you attend will provide all the necessary equipment. Once you're hooked, you'll want to look into buying your own microlight (prices average between £10,000–£40,000).

There is a good second-hand market for microlights (prices start at £3000 for reasonable models), but do take proper advice and research thoroughly before buying. If buying your own craft is not an option, then you could consider joining a syndicate through your local club or setting one up with other pilots. This shares the costs, making the sport much more affordable.

WHERE TO GET INVOLVED

ADMINISTRATIVE BODIES

British Microlight Aircraft Association (BMAA)
www.bmaa.org
01869 338888
BMAA, The Bullring, Deddington, Banbury, Oxfordshire OX15 0TT

The British Microlight Aircraft Association looks after the interests of microlight owners in the UK. Approved by the Civil Aviation Authority (CAA), its aims are to further the sport of microlight aviation, to keep flying costs to a minimum for its members, and to represent members in national and international matters relating to the sport.

CLUBS AND COMMERCIAL SCHOOLS

In line with the sport's huge popularity, there are many microlighting organisations around the UK. Commercial schools are affiliated with clubs so there is a wealth of places for you to seek good advice on the sport and receive training. A full listing is available on the BMAA's website (go to www.bmaa.org/clubs.asp); we have listed some of them here.

South-east and London

Airbourne Aviation Ltd & The Microlight Aviation Club
www.flyMAC.co.uk
0845 130 9676
Popham Airfield, Hampshire

Cloudbase Aviation School
www.theflyingschool.co.uk
01737 822423
Cloudbase Aviation Services Limited, Redhill Aerodrome, Crab Hill Lane, South Nutfield, Surrey RH1 5JY

Hampshire Microlight Club
www.hmfclub.com
023 9246 8806/078 3475 2083
Colemore Common, Petersfield, Hampshire

Medway Microlights & Medway Airsports Club
www.ravenmad.co.uk
01634 270236
Burrows Lane, Middle Stoke, Rochester, Kent ME3 9RN

Solent Microlights
www.flyingschool.com
01983 402402
Isle of Wight Airport, Embassy Way, Sandown, Isle of Wight PO36 0JP

South-west

Cornwall Flying Club
www.cornwallflyingclub.com
01208 821419
Cornwall Flying Club Ltd, Bodmin Airfield, Cardinham, Bodmin, Cornwall PL30 4BU
E-mail: fly@cornwallflyingclub.com

WHERE TO GET INVOLVED

GS Aviation Europe Ltd
www.gsaviation.co.uk
01672 515535
Clench Common Airfield,
Clench Common, Marlborough,
Wiltshire SN6 4NZ

Kemble Flying Club & Pegasus Flight Training (Cotswolds)
www.kembleflyingclub.co.uk
01285 770077
E-mail:
enquiries@kembleflyingclub.co.uk
Kemble Airfield, Cirencester,
Gloucestershire GL7 6BA

Redlands Airfield
www.redlandsairfield.co.uk
01793 791014
Redlands Airfield Ltd, Redlands
Farm, Wanborough, Swindon,
Wiltshire SN4 0AA

Somerset Microlights & Devon and Somerset Microlight Club
www.somerset-microlights.com
01404 891880
Somerset Microlights, Dunkeswell
Airfield, Honiton, Devon EX14 4LJ

Swallow Aviation
www.swallowaviation.co.uk
01747 838642

The Wiltshire Microlight Centre & Wiltshire Microlight Club
www.wiltsmicrolights.com
07836 554554

Wales and West Midlands

The Microlight School
www.microlightschool.org.uk
01283 792193
Roddige Airfield, Roddige Lane, Nr
Lichfield, Staffordshire WS13 8QS

Microlight Wales
www.microlightwales.co.uk
0208 1443 633/07734 428 144
Email: office@microlightwales.co.uk

Midland Microlights
www.midlandmicrolights.co.uk
01283 716265/07802 728051
Catholme Lane, Barton under
Needwood, Burton-on-Trent,
Staffordshire DE13 8DA

East Midlands

Airways Airsports
www.airways-airsports.com
01335 344308
Darley Moor Airfield, Ashbourne,
Derbyshire DE6 2ET
E-mail: office@airways-airsports.com

Fly365 Ltd
www.fly365.co.uk
07831 439651
The Old Control Tower, Wickenby
Airfield, Langworth, Lincoln LN3 5AX
E-mail: info@fly365.co.uk

WHERE TO GET INVOLVED

Northampton Microlight Club
www.northamptonmicrolightclub.org.uk
01908 371 714

Skylight Aviation School & Robin Hood Microlight Club
0115 960 7600/07764 253394

East of England

Bedford Microlight Centre
www.bedfordmicrolightcentre.co.uk
01767 691616
E-mail:
info@bedfordmicrolightcentre.co.uk

AAA Chatteris Microlight Flight Training
aaa.microlight.com
07834 977555/01487 843333
AAA Microlights, Chatteris Airfield, Cambridgeshire PE150 EA
E-mail: info@aaamicrolight.com

Nene Valley Microlights
www.nenevalleymicrolights.co.uk
01933 311895
Sackville Farm, Riseley, Bedfordshire, MK44 1BS

Northern England

Airsports Training
www.airsportstraining.co.uk
01904 738877
Rufforth Airfield East, York YO23 3QA
E-mail: info@airsportstraining.co.uk

Cheshire Microlight Centre
www.cheshiremicrolights.co.uk
01270 764713/07831 274201
E-mail:
enquire@cheshiremicrolights.co.uk

Cumbria Microlight Training Centre
www.cumbria-microlight-training.co.uk
07711 064851/01228 526461
Based at Carlisle Airport
E-mail: cumbria-microlight-training@cmt.co.uk

Flyrite (near Lancaster)
www.flyrite.net
01282 436280/07946 547342
E-mail: flylonsdale@yahoo.co.uk

Mainair Microlight School
www.mainairflyingschool.co.uk
0161 787 9034
Mainair Flying School, Barton Aerodrome, Liverpool Road, Eccles, Manchester M30 7SA

Northern Microlights
www.northernmicrolights.co.uk
01995 641058
E-mail: northernmicros@aol.com

Northumbrian Microlights
www.northumbrianmicrolights.co.uk
01670 787067/07798 771415
The Airfield, Bockenfield, Nr Felton, Northumberland

AIR

WHERE TO GET INVOLVED

Scotland

East of Scotland Microlights
www.eosm.co.uk
01875 820102

Grampian Microlight Flying Club
www.gmfc-insch.co.uk
01464 820003
Insch Airfield, Auchleven, Insch,
Aberdeenshire AB52 6PL

Microlight Scotland
www.microlightscotland.com
0797 997 1301
Strathaven Airfield, Lethame Road,
Strathaven ML10 6RW
E-mail: fly@microlightscotland.com

Pegasus Flight Training Scotland
www.samd.co.uk
01738 550044/07802 481285
Perth Airport, Nr Scone, Perth PH2 6PL
E-mail: info@samd.co.uk

Richard Cook Microlight Training School
www.microlighttrainingscotland.com
07787 518662/0141 942 2804
E-mail:
richard@microlighttrainingscotland.com

Northern Ireland

Fly NI Air Sports
www.flyni.co.uk
0845 0940189/07747 806029
E-mail: fly@flyni.co.uk

08 PARACHUTING AND FREEFALLING

BUZZ FOR YOUR BUCK 2/10

THRILL FACTOR

'Skydiving is much more than jumping out of an aeroplane – it's the closest thing to real human flight imaginable. Becoming World Champions in this incredible sport is something we always dreamed of; but then, so is human flight.'

***Emma Beyer**, UK National and Women's Skydiving Team*

For some bizarre and perverse reason, Brits put throwing themselves out of perfectly safe aeroplanes at the top of their list of preferred adventure sports. (Draw your own conclusions!) But perhaps this appetite for danger is not so perverse when you consider that parachuting and freefalling offer total mastery of the air and the freedom to make the sky your own. This is an exhilarating sport for the absolute beginner. It is also a highly competitive sport that requires dedication, finely-tuned skills, excellent understanding of the air and perfect body control.

If this is not sufficient enough a challenge for you, then once you're proficient in freefalling there's always skysurfing to be mastered. Skysurfers are basically skydivers wearing boards attached to their feet and performing surfing-style aerobatics during freefall. Skysurfing is an incredible skill that requires considerable practice.

THE UK NATIONAL AND WOMEN'S SKYDIVING TEAM (PHOTOGRAPHER: ANDY WRIGHT)

For those who are happy to tackle parachuting in the first instance, then prepare your nerves and bodily functions for an experience of a lifetime.

The record for the highest parachute jump is held by Captain Joe Kittinger. In 1960 he jumped from an altitude of 31 km (102,800 feet). His freefall lasted 4 minutes 36 seconds, during which time he approached speeds of up to 988 km/h (614 miles per hour), almost breaking the sound barrier. Come on, isn't it time to challenge a record that hasn't been broken for over 40 years and make history? (Incidentally, it was a dog who first tried parachuting, in 1785, when his owner, Jean Pierre Blanchard, of hot air ballooning fame, volunteered his four-legged friend for the challenge.)

GETTING INVOLVED

Different clubs operate different height/weight restrictions, so check before you book and/or travel. A medical declaration will be required and, if you're over 40 years of age, you'll need to complete a BPA medical form from the centre where you're jumping, to be signed by your GP. If you are under eighteen, you'll need a signed parental consent form. The principal medical restrictions are diabetes, epilepsy, fits, recurrent blackouts, heart or lung disease, mental illness and, in some cases, asthma.

GETTING STARTED

Arguably the best, cheapest and quickest way to make your first jump is static line parachuting. This is when your parachute opens automatically as you leave the aircraft. After just six hours of training you could be flying up to between 670–1070 metres (2200 and 3500 feet) and jumping. There are two options – Static Line Rounds or Static Line Squares, or Ram Air Progression System (RAPS). With Static Line Rounds the parachute is circular and has very little forward velocity giving the sensation of floating gently to the ground. The Static Line Squares, or RAPS, allow you to jump with a square canopy on your first jump. This system enables you to break and turn and offers softer landings, with the additional knowledge that if you want to take the sport further you will be using the same equipment.

TAKING IT FURTHER

Some people want to experience the unforgettable adrenaline buzz of Accelerated Freefall (AFF), and this is your third option. You normally make your first descent from 3.7 km (12,000 feet), accompanied by two highly specialised instructors who guide you in freefall by way of hand signals and radio communication. You will experience between 40 and 45 seconds of freefall before you open your canopy at 1.5 km (5000 feet).

Your first AFF jump will usually be part of a week's course of 8–10 jumps. An Accelerated Freefall Course will set you back upwards of £1200, but this is the quickest way to get a skydiving licence and probably the most exhilarating. Once qualified, jumps can be made for as little as £15, depending on the club – which is a lot of 'Buzz for Your Buck'!

If you are tempted by freefall, but want to rise to the challenge more gradually, then the fourth option is a tandem parachute jump. For this, you will be securely attached to an experienced tandem instructor who will take care of vital functions, such as opening the parachute and landing safely. Your preparation for the jump takes only 15 minutes. Weather permitting, you exit the aircraft from around 3 km (10,000 feet) and experience 30 seconds of freefall before your instructor deploys the parachute. Freed from responsibility, you can relax and enjoy the experience of rushing towards the earth.

With all of the above options, the best way to start parachuting is via a club or centre.

EQUIPMENT NEEDED

For one-off jumps, the centre or club you're jumping with will provide all the kit you need. You simply have to turn up sensibly dressed and feeling brave.

Once you've built up some experience, buying your first complete rig can be the beginning of a new and exciting relationship. Given the choice available this can be daunting, so take lots of advice and prepare to make a fairly significant dent in your bank balance. A complete set of brand-new custom equipment that includes main, reserve, rig and automatic activation device (AAD) will cost anywhere between £2500 and £3500. But there is also plenty of good second-hand equipment available, so do your research carefully.

In addition to your rig, you'll need a well-fitted jumpsuit. These tend to be custom made, so allow time for this process. An altimeter is a mandatory piece of skydiving equipment that records altitude; look for one that you find easy to read. Helmets are also mandatory. Make sure that your helmet is not only safe but comfortable; take time to find the perfect fit.

WHERE TO GET INVOLVED

ADMINISTRATIVE BODIES

British Parachuting Association
www.bpa.org.uk
0116 278 5271
5 Wharf Way, Glen Parva,
Leicester LE2 9TF
E-mail: skydive@bpa.org.uk

The British Parachute Association (BPA) was founded in 1962 to organise, govern and further the advancement of Sport Parachuting within the UK. The Association's aim today is to encourage participation and promote excellence at all levels of skydiving, from novice to world-class competitor. Below is a list of BPA-affiliated parachute clubs and centres around the UK.

WHERE TO GET INVOLVED

CLUBS AND COMMERCIAL SCHOOLS

South-east

Headcorn Parachute Club
www.headcornparachuteclub.co.uk
01622 890862
Headcorn Airfield, Headcorn, Nr Ashford, Kent TN27 9HX

London Parachute School
www.londonparachuteschool.com
0845 130 7194
The Byre, Woods Farm, Easthampstead Road, Wokingham, Berkshire RG40 3AE
E-mail: info@londonparachuteschool.com

Skydive Weston
www.skydiveweston.com
01869 343201
RAF Weston on the Green, Bicester, Oxfordshire OX25 3TQ
E-mail: skydiveweston@fsmail.net

South-west

Army Parachute Association at Netheravon
www.netheravon.com
01980 678250
Army Parachute Association, Airfield Camp, Netheravon, Wiltshire SP4 9SF
E-mail: info@netheravon.com

Cornish Parachute Club
www.cornishparachuteclub.co.uk
01872 553352/07790 439653
Perranporth Airfield, Higher Trevallas, St Agnes, Cornwall TR5 0XS
E-mail: cornishparachuteclub@hotmail.co.uk

Devon and Somerset Parachute School
www.parachuting-uk.com
01884 250480/07718 638000
South West Air Activities, 19 Lime Road, Tiverton, Devon
E-mail: info@parachuting-uk.com

Skydive London
www.skydivelondon.co.uk
01793 791222
Redlands Farm, Wanborough, Swindon, Wiltshire SN4 0AA
E-mail: info@skydivelondon.co.uk

Wales and West Midlands

The Parachute Centre
www.theparachutecentre.com
01948 841111
Tilstock Airfield, Whitchurch, Shropshire SY13 2HA

East Midlands

British Parachute School Ltd
www.bpslangar.co.uk
01949 860878
The Control Tower, Langar Airfield, Langar Nottingham NG13 9HY
E-mail: info@bpslangar.co.uk

Hinton Skydiving Centre
www.skydive.co.uk
01295 812300
Hinton Airfield, Steane, Brackley, Northamptonshire NN13 5NS
E-mail: info@skydive.co.uk

WHERE TO GET INVOLVED

East of England

Peterborough Parachute Centre
www.skydivesibson.com
01832 280490
Skydive Sibson, Peterborough Parachute Centre, Wansford, Peterborough PE8 6NE
E-mail: skydivesibson@btconnect.com

UK Parachuting
www.ukparachuting.co.uk
01953 861030
Buckenham Airfield, Old Buckenham, Norfolk

Northern England

Black Knights Parachute Centre
www.bkpc.co.uk
01772 717624
43 Garstone Croft, Preston, Lancashire PR2 3WY
E-mail: info@bkpc.co.uk

British Skysports
www.britishskysports.co.uk
01262 677367
East Leys Farm, Grindale Road, Bridlington, East Yorkshire YO16 4YB

North West Parachute Centre
www.skydive-northwest.com
Cark Airfield, Flookburgh, Grange Over Sands, Cumbria LA11 7LS
01539 558672

Peterlee Parachute Centre
www.skydiveacademy.org.uk
0191 517 1234 / 07000 586785
Skydive Academy, Peterlee Parachute Centre, PO Box 192, Durham DH1 5WD
E-mail:
enquiries@skydiveacademy.org.uk

Target Skysports
www.skydiving.co.uk
0113 250 5600
Hibaldstow Airfield, Nr Brigg, North Lincs, CN20 9NN (dropzone)

Scotland

Paragon Skydiving Club
www.paragonskydiving.co.uk
01821 642454
Errol Airfield, Grange, Perthshire PH2 7TB

Skydive St Andrews
www.skydivestandrews.co.uk
01334 880678
Kingsmuir Airfield, Fife KY16 8QQ
E-mail: mail@skydivestandrews.co.uk

Skydive Strathallan
www.skydivestrathallan.co.uk
0176 4662572 (weekends only)
Skydive Strathallan, Strathallan Airfield, Nr Auchterarder, Perthshire PH3 1LA

Northern Ireland

Wild Geese Parachute Centre
www.skydivewildgeese.com
028 2955 8609
Movenis Airfield, Carrowreagh Road, Garvagh, Co. Londonderry BT51 5LQ
E-mail: wild.geese@btconnect.com

09 PARAGLIDING

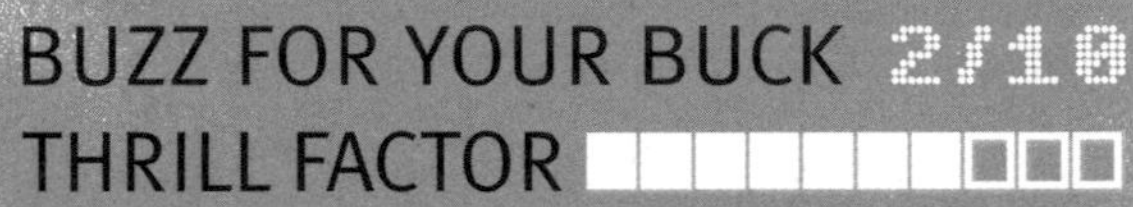

> 'Born out of passion, paragliding is an obsession, a life changing experience. Once you've taken those first steps into your new world, you'll long to return again and again.'

***Dean Crosby**, former British Champion*

Have you ever longed to fly like a bird? As a child, did you dream of flying like Peter Pan, if only for a day? Personal flight is the realisation of one of humanity's oldest and greatest dreams. So, why not take to the skies with a paraglider and live the dream?

A paraglider is a very light flexible wing, sharing many of the characteristics of a parachute (from which it was developed). As the pilot, you are clipped into a harness and adopt a comfortable sitting position with your legs dangling free.

Once attached to the paraglider, you run down a gentle slope and – in theory and after a bit of practice – glide gracefully away. There is no freefalling or jumping off cliffs. The launches and landings are slow and gentle (with practice), but when in the air you'll need to have your wits about you and your senses on high alert. As with hang gliding, your motor is the silent thermals and air currents that can carry you up and away – although when you're starting out, you'll be ridge soaring before 'graduating' to the excitement of thermal flying. Once you're riding a thermal, be prepared to descend at a rate of about 60 metres (200 feet) per minute until you find your next thermal to soar on. The frustration of paragliding can be canopy collapses, caused by rough air and the fact that the wing is unsupported by a metal frame. However, experts reassure us that, with tuition and practice, canopy collapses can usually be controlled by using the brakes. In the true adventure sport spirit, we prefer to see this as a challenge to be overcome rather than a source of frustration!

During training, you will simply skim the ground to start with, but as your confidence and skills grow you'll soar higher and higher and be out there for longer and longer. Experienced paraglider pilots can routinely stay airborne for 3 hours or more; the duration record stands at over 11 hours. British paraglider pilot Robbie Whittall set a World Record when he soared to nearly 4.5 km (15,000 feet), and the distance record is over 400 km (250 miles).

One final word on this sport: trees. Watch out for them. Landing in trees is an occupational hazard of paragliding, and un-knitting a paraglider from a tree is a very time-consuming business (providing your friends with ample time to get their cameras out and record your tree-hugging antics for posterity and amusement).

GETTING INVOLVED

Paragliding is about finesse and serenity, not strength and adrenaline. General athletic ability helps as paragliding requires an amount of hiking to reach your starting point, but once you're in the air the physical effort is minimal. Being overweight and out of shape will put you at a disadvantage when hiking (although you can drive to many flying sites), but once airborne it can often help to be a bit heavier. There is no age limit – you just need to be alert to potential hazards and exercise common sense. However, it's important to have the maturity to respect the hazards. Paraglider pilots range from teenagers through to seventy-year-old seasoned aviators.

PARAGLIDING: NOT JUST THE BEST SEAT IN THE HOUSE, BUT THE BEST SEAT IN THE WORLD

GETTING STARTED

Wannabe buzzards can try a taster day. This will teach you how to take off and land safely, as well as give you several solo flights. This should be more than enough to get you hooked. Taster days cost from around £125, with some including the cost of day membership to the British Hang Gliding and Paragliding Association.

If you want to break yourself in even more gently, then try parascending. For this, you'll be towed behind a 4x4 or a boat. It's certainly the simplest and quickest ways to get a taste for flying free.

TAKING IT FURTHER

If you want to develop your paragliding skills further, there are four levels you can aim for:

- Elementary pilot
- Club pilot
- Pilot
- Advanced pilot.

An Elementary Paragliding Course (EPC) will set you back about £500 and usually lasts for 5 days. A Club Pilot Course costs about the same; you will need to be EPC-qualified first. Some centres offer all-inclusive courses to take you from absolute beginner to flying solo; you should expect to pay upwards of £850 for these.

EQUIPMENT NEEDED

As a beginner, a club or school will provide you with the paraglider, harness, helmet and radio. No special clothing is required, although full-length trousers and running shoes with ankle support are advisable. Once you decide to buy your own equipment, budget around £1700 for a new wing suitable for beginners. A new paraglider suitable for a recently trained pilot will cost up to £2000; second-hand canopies can be bought for much less, but expect to pay £500 or more. The average useful life of a paraglider is 3–4 years, but this does depend on the amount of use and exposure to UV. If you're buying second-hand equipment, make sure to research thoroughly before buying. Find out how long wings have been in use for and in what conditions.

Harnesses are an essential piece of kit and will cost £400 or more. When deciding which sort to buy, be guided by your school and instructor. A harness fitted with an airbag is highly recommended for 'less than elegant' landings! The best bet is to try out a few harnesses at your club and talk to pilots about their views before buying. Other recommended kit includes gloves with thermal lining, sturdy boots with ankle support and a helmet.

WHERE TO GET INVOLVED

ADMINISTRATIVE BODIES

The British Hang Gliding and Paragliding Association (BHPA)
www.bhpa.co.uk
0116 261 1322
The Old School Room, Loughborough Road, Leicester LE4 5PJ
E-mail: office@bhpa.co.uk

The BHPA covers hang gliding, paragliding, parascending and paramotoring, and has over 9000 members across the country.

The Scottish Hang Gliding and Paragliding Federation
www.flyingscot.f9.co.uk
01355 246252

REGIONAL CLUBS AND SCHOOLS

There are many BHPA-registered clubs around the country; you'll find a full listing on the BHPA website (www.bhpa.co.uk/bhpa/clubs/index.php). We've listed some of the clubs below. Paragliding clubs look after flying sites and offer a supportive flying and social environment. They do not provide basic training.

If you are a beginner and want to find training or a trial flight, you should contact one of the BHPA-registered schools or call up your nearest club and ask them to recommend a school. We've listed some of the schools (see below); a full listing can be found at www.bhpa.co.uk/bhpa/schools/index.php.

South-east and London

CLUBS:

Dunstable Hang Gliding and Paragliding
www.dhpc.info
0208 367 8068

Sky Surfing Club
www.skysurfingclub.co.uk
(Petersfield area of Hampshire and West Sussex)

AIR

WHERE TO GET INVOLVED

SCHOOLS:
Green Dragons Airsports Academy
www.greendragons.co.uk
01883 652666
Warren Barn Farm, Slines Oak Road,
Woldingham, Surrey CR3 7HN

Sussex Paragliding School
www.flysussex.com
01273 858170
FlySussex.com, Tollgate, Beddington,
Nr Lewes, East Sussex BN8 6JZ
E-mail: info@flysussex.com

South-west
CLUBS:
Avon Hang Gliding and Paragliding Club
www.avonhgpg.co.uk
E-mail: membership@avonhgpg.co.uk

Devon and Somerset Condors
www.dscondors.co.uk
01392 204253

Kernow Hang Gliding and Paragliding Association (Cornwall)
www.khpa.co.uk
01872 273839

Thames Valley Hang Gliding and Paragliding Club (Wiltshire)
www.tvhgc.co.uk
01344 872266
E-mail: membership@tvhgc.co.uk

Wessex Hang Gliding and Paragliding Club
www.wessexhgpg.org.uk
01202 311574
E-mail: secretary@wessexhgpc.org.uk

SCHOOLS:
Southwest Paragliding School
www.paragliding-school.co.uk
01822 810532/07973 924963
'Cranmere', Mary Tavy, Tavistock,
Devon PL19 9QB
E-mail: innes@paragliding-school.co.uk

Wales and West Midlands
CLUBS:
Long Mynd Soaring Club (Shropshire and East Wales)
www.longmynd.org
E-mail: membership@longmynd.org

Malvern Hang Gliding Club
www.malvern-hang.org.uk
07773 493 622

North Wales Hang Gliding and Paragliding Club
www.nwhgpc.org.uk

The South-east Wales Hang Gliding and Paragliding Club
www.sewhgpgc.co.uk
01656 648246

WHERE TO GET INVOLVED

SCHOOLS:

Paraventure Airsport
www.paraventure.co.uk
01873 881127/07775 865095

Snowdon Gliders
www.snowdongliders.co.uk
01248 600330

The Mountain Paragliding Centre
Yr Ynys, Mynydd Llandegai, Bangor, Gwynedd, North Wales LL57 4BZ

Welsh Hang Gliding and Paragliding Centre
www.welshairsports.com
01873 854090/0791 4026004
Welsh Airsports, Wilberton House, Frogmore Street, Abergavenny NP7 5AL

East Midlands

CLUBS:

Derbyshire Soaring Club
www.derbyshiresoaringclub.org.uk
0709 2017770

SCHOOLS:

Airways Airsports
www.airways-airsports.com
01335 344308
Darley Moor Airfield, Ashbourne, Derbyshire DE6 2ET
E-mail: office@airways-airsports.com

Derbyshire Flying Centre
www.d-f-c.co.uk
0845 108 1577/01298 872313

East of England

CLUBS:

Norfolk Hang Gliding and Paragliding Club
www.flynorfolk.co.uk

Northern England

CLUBS:

Dales Hang Gliding and Paragliding Club
www.dhpc.org.uk
07720 425146
E-mail: contacts@dhpc.org.uk

Northumbria Hang Gliding and Paragliding Club
www.nhpc.org.uk
0191 523 6886/01661 842166

Pennine Soaring Club
www.penninesoaringclub.org.uk
E-mail:
secretary@penninesoaringclub.org.uk

SCHOOLS:

Airventures Paragliding School
www.airventures.co.uk
07830 281986
Keswick Climbing Wall, Southey Hill, Keswick, Cumbria CA12 5NR

Scotland

CLUBS:

Aberdeen Hang Gliding and Paragliding Club
www.ahpc.org.uk
01224 326095

WHERE TO GET INVOLVED

Lanarkshire and Lothian Soaring Club
www.llsclub.org.uk
E-mail: info@llsclub.org.uk

SCHOOLS:
Cloudbusters
www.cloudbusters.co.uk
07899 878509

Flying Fever
www.flyingfever.net
01770 820292/07984 356149
No 2 Coastguard House, Kildonan, Isle of Arran, Scotland
E-mail: mail@flyingfever.net

Northern Ireland
CLUBS:
The Ulster Hang Gliding and Paragliding Club
www.uhpc.f9.co.uk
028 3834 1544/07729 549163
E-mail: secretary@uhpc.f9.co.uk

SCHOOLS:
Aerosports
www.aerosports.co.uk
02893 341414/07879 632111
E-mail: ken@aerosports.co.uk

First Flight Paragliding School (Belfast)
028 9083 2648

10

SCAD DIVING

OFF THE RATINGS!

For any adrenaline-addicted people who think that taking a pit bull terrier for a stroll in the park is more daring than bungee jumping, we've got a new challenge for you. Leave your pit bull at home, get down to the nearest SCAD diving site and be prepared to be winched aloft in a crane and dropped from a height of about 50 metres (160 feet) into a net below. No lines, no cords, no elastic.

Named SCAD diving after the Suspended Catch Air Device (SCAD) that you land in, this sport offers the ultimate 100 per cent freefall and acceleration experience, and all at an affordable price. With a drop that's three times longer than an average bungee jump, you'll experience great acceleration and a buzz you'll struggle to get elsewhere for the same price.

A newcomer to the adventure sports scene, the German-invented SCAD diving is proving to be a real adrenaline-fuelled success.

GETTING INVOLVED

GETTING STARTED

Age is no limit when it comes to SCAD diving. As long as you weigh between 49–150 kg (7 stone 11 lb and 23 stone 8 lb), are not pregnant and are free from medical conditions including heart conditions, high blood pressure, back problems and epilepsy, then SCAD diving is for you. Prices vary from site to site, but budget to spend up to £50. This might seem expensive for a two-second fall, but trust us – you won't regret a penny of it.

TAKING IT FURTHER

You can either choose to SCAD dive all over the world (the experience won't be hugely different each time, but the backdrop will vary dramatically) or you can get involved with companies that have special effects teams that design and co-ordinate performances and stunts for advertising campaigns, television and show productions, theatres and circuses.

3 . . . 2 . . . 1 . . . DIVE!

EQUIPMENT NEEDED

You won't need to turn up to the site with any equipment, just sensible clothing. You will be provided with a harness and knee pads. Then, all you have to do is gather your courage and wait until the crane is ready to hoist you up.

WHERE TO GET INVOLVED

ADMINISTRATIVE BODIES

British Elastic Rope Sports Association (BERSA)
www.bungeezone.com/orgs/bersa.shtml
01865 311179
33a Canal Street, Oxford OX2 6BQ

The British Elastic Rope Sports Association (BERSA) exists to promote safety by regulation of the sport in the UK. BERSA is responsible for ensuring the highest standards of safety are maintained at certified clubs, and for training and licensing their staff. Furthermore, because BERSA is a non-profit-making body, it is able to act as a centre of expertise, encouraging an on-going programme of research and development of the sport.

COMPANIES

Dropzone UK
www.dropzoneuk.com

Dropzone UK has the only mobile SCAD system in the UK. Check out their website for locations near you.

The UK Bungee Club
www.ukbungee.co.uk
07000 286 433

This is the largest bungee club in the UK and offers SCAD diving in locations across the country. Check out the website (www.ukbungee.co.uk) for dates and locations. Pre-booking is essential.

LAND

TOP 5 LAND SPORTS BY 'BUZZ FOR YOUR BUCK'

Rank	Sport
1	Mountain boarding
2	Mountain biking
3	Caving
4	Abseiling, freefall rappelling, rap jumping
5	Kite landboarding, kite buggying, buggy jumping

TOP 5 LAND SPORTS BY 'THRILL FACTOR'

Rank	Sport
1	Karting
2	Kite landboarding, kite buggying, buggy jumping
3	Land yachting
4	Abseiling, freefall rappelling, rap jumping
5	Mountain biking

11

ABSEILING, FREEFALL RAPPELLING, RAP JUMPING

BUZZ FOR YOUR BUCK 8/10
THRILL FACTOR ■■■■■■□□□□

If abseiling, or rappelling, brings to mind deeply unglamorous thoughts of sweaty anoraks, practice walls in a smelly school gym or a wet weekend at an outward bound centre in Wales, then think again. Think Angelina Jolie as she abseils down a New York skyscraper before casually flagging down a cab in the film *Mr & Mrs Smith*; think 007 and Pierce Brosnan as he rappels over a concrete chasm in the opening scenes of *Goldeneye*; and, if you're still not convinced, then turn your mind to Lara Croft rappelling upside down off a cliff while shooting at the bad guys. That should do it. That should make you reach for the nearest karabiner you can find and crave some serious rope action.

Derived from the German word abseil (ab- meaning 'to go down' and -seil meaning 'rope'), abseiling was originally developed by rock climbers and mountaineers to descend cliffs and mountains safely. Today, it is a hugely popular adventure sport in the UK. The adrenaline rush as you conquer your fear of heights and skilfully reach the ground in the second-quickest way possible (after freefall), is what keeps devotees going back for more.

One extremely good reason for taking up abseiling is the wider range of sports it will open up to you. You'll find abseiling techniques are used not only in rock climbing (to return to the base of a climb or try a new route) but also in canyoning (where you may find yourself descending mountainous watercourses, waterfalls or cliffs), and even caving.

Once you've cracked abseiling, you might want to try freefall rappelling or freefall abseiling. So, what's the difference? Err . . . there's no wall, you just descend daringly down a rope. Freefall rappelling is a technique used in sports such as caving, as it allows you to descend in areas where there are no walls. It's a skill used by people who want to really push themselves, do it faster and even do it face down! In terms of pulling power, it'll put you up there with the world's Special Forces, who use freefall rappelling as a very aggressive method of deployment into buildings and on to the ground from helicopters.

Rap jumping is another whole kettle of abseiling fish. If climbing down the sides of a cliff on a rope isn't enough of a thrill for you, and even doing it freefall without the cliff doesn't get your heart racing, why not go over the edge head first and run? Deemed an extreme sport and a serious challenge, rap jumping involves going over the edge head first, facing the precipice and walking, jogging or running down the mountain. Plunging headfirst down a

ABSEILING: THE ONLY WAY IS DOWN!

cliff is guaranteed to give you the required adrenaline rush and a pretty good pub story to boot. But you'll have to be convincing – people might not believe you've done anything quite this extreme.

GETTING INVOLVED

You don't need any previous experience to start abseiling. Centres around the country offer 1-day abseiling courses, which will give you a good introduction and help you decide if you want to take it further. You'll learn about cliff line safety, the proper abseiling technique, correct use of the Figure-of-eight descender, pre-abseil checks, standard calls, and braking and belaying techniques. Expect to pay around £80 for a 1-day course. These centres will also be able to give you advice on taking it further with freefall rapelling and, if you're crazy enough, rap jumping.

EQUIPMENT NEEDED

You don't need any specialised equipment to get started. By joining an organised course, the centre will provide all the equipment you need. All you need to do is wear clothes that you don't mind getting dirty or spoiling. It's also essential to wear footwear that has a good grip.

ABSEILING: THE FUN WAY TO DROP IN ON FRIENDS?

WHERE TO GET INVOLVED

ADMINISTRATIVE BODIES

British Mountaineering Council (BMC)
www.thebmc.co.uk
0870 0104878

The British Mountaineering Council (BMC) is the representative body that exists to protect the freedoms and promote the interests of climbers, hill walkers and mountaineers. The BMC's website lists clubs across the UK, and the Regional Access Database will give you lots of information about your local crag, for example, access, birds nesting, etc.

Mountaineering Council of Scotland
www.mountaineering-scotland.org.uk
01738 493942

CLUBS AND SOCIETIES

Get in touch with a club near you and they'll be able to recommend the nearby climbing facilities that they use and where you'll be able to have lessons. Taking advice from experienced and enthusiastic climbers is vital and will be the best way to help you find a place to learn that's right for you.

You'll also find an area on the BMC website that allows you to search for local and national clubs. We've listed many of those clubs below.

South-east and London

Chelmsford Mountaineering Club
www.chelmsfordmountainclub.co.uk
enquiry@chelmsfordmountainclub.co.uk

Hertfordshire Mountaineering Club
www.thehmc.co.uk
chairman@thehmc.co.uk

Maidstone Mountaineering Club
www.mmce.co.uk

Marylebone Mountaineering Club
www.themmc.org.uk

Meadhurst Mountaineering Club
www.meadhurstmc.org.uk

Reading Mountaineering Club
www.readingmountaineeringclub.org.uk
01494 533828

Slough Mountaineering Club
www.slough-mountaineering.org.uk

Surbiton & Kingston Mt Club
www.sakmc.org
sakmc@hotmail.com

South-west

Gloucestershire Mountaineering Club
www.thegmc.org.uk
MembershipSecretary@thegmc.org.uk

Wales and West Midlands

Clwyd Mountaineering Club
www.clwydmountaineeringclub.co.uk
01248 355985

WHERE TO GET INVOLVED

Gwent Mountaineering Club
www.gwentmountaineeringclub.
org.uk
02920 852771

Mercian Mountaineering Club
www.mercianmc.co.uk
07876 751557

Rugby Mountaineering Club
www.rugbymc.uklinux.net
01788 890777

Solihull Mountaineering Club
www.solihullmc.org.uk
membership@solihullmc.org.uk

East Midlands

Clogwyn Mountaineering Club
www.clogwyn.org.uk
01283 734126

Northern England

Carlisle Mountaineering Club
www.freetimeonline.co.uk/CMC/Index
.cfm

Eden Valley Mountaineering Club
www.evmc.co.uk
01768 866082

Scotland

Braes O'Fife Mountaineering Club
www.braesofife.org.uk
01592 599051

Cairn Ban Mountaineering Club
www.acairnban.org.uk
07717 298556

12 ADVENTURE RACING

BUZZ FOR YOUR BUCK 7/10
THRILL FACTOR

'It's not about the winning, it's about the taking part.' That's what my parents used to say to me when I'd lost the egg and spoon race, come last in the wheelbarrow race and fallen out of my sack in the sack race. I didn't believe them for a second. But now I've found a sport where it really can be all about the taking part: adventure racing.

Adventure racing has become hugely popular in the UK. And it's no wonder, since this sport combines two or more disciplines and encourages team entries. The disciplines typically include orienteering and navigation, cross-country running, mountain biking, paddling, climbing and related rope skills. Short races might last a few hours; longer races can last up to 10 days or more, during which time the teams must choose when (and if) to rest.

There are many races held all over the UK throughout the year. One of the better-known races is the Rat Race, which takes place in Bristol, Edinburgh and Manchester. Teams of three people have to run, climb, mountain bike, abseil and kayak the streets, structures and waterways of a course that's only revealed to the racers a few hours before the start. Furthermore, to keep the racers on their toes, there are a number of 'Rat Trap' surprise challenges along the route. What better fun and physical challenge could you ask for in one weekend? And, if you're worried you'll be missing a Saturday night out, think of all the celebrating there is to do with your fellow teammates when you cross the finishing line. . .

Another big plus point for adventure racing is that each race is so different. Not only are locations varied, making the challenges of each race unique, but the formats also differ. As a beginner you might find yourself tackling a 4-hour mountain bike orienteering race in the Yorkshire Dales, but with this under your belt you might want to tackle a race of 2 hours of running, 3 hours of mountain biking and 1 hour of night navigation on the South Downs. Most races have check points (CPs) along the route; by visiting these you accumulate team points (CPs have different values depending on their location). The team that accumulates the most points in the shortest time wins. But, as we said, it's not about the winning. . .

GETTING INVOLVED

You don't need to be super-human to compete in an adventure race, but you do need to attain a certain level of fitness, which you will reach with consistent training in the run up to a race. As it's a team sport, try training with your fellow team members; not only will this give the whole team encouragement and support when individual members feel like flagging, it will also help you to learn about each other's strengths and weaknesses.

GETTING STARTED

You will probably start by entering sprint races, which last from 3–6 hours, covering distances from 32–48 km (20–30 miles). Break this down and you'll be mountain biking for 16–24 km (10–15 miles), running for 6–16 km (4–10 miles) and paddling for 3–8 km (2–5 miles).

TAKING IT FURTHER

Once you've got the bug, you might want to enter endurance races of 4 to 12 hours, 24-hour races, multi-day races from 36 hours to 4 days, or expedition races from 4 days onwards. For the longer races you'll be navigating,

MOUNTAIN BIKING: ANNE CAROLINE CHAUSSON MAKES TRACKS IN A DOWNHILL TIME TRIAL

orienteering and probably using rope skills for rappelling, etc. For expedition races you may be faced with additional disciplines such as horse riding and extensive mountaineering.

Is a seven-stage foot race through the Amazon rainforest up your street? If the thought of the bugs or heat puts you off, how about the 740 km (460-mile) Yukon Arctic Ultra? No bugs, no heat, just some of the most hostile and demanding terrain you could hope to conquer. Go on, you know you want to.

EQUIPMENT NEEDED

The equipment you need will vary from race to race, every race is different. Race organisers will give you a definitive list of what you need to compete, and there will usually be mandatory equipment checks and standards that must be met. If you're worried in the first instance that the amount of kit you need is going to be prohibitive, don't be – many race organisers hire out equipment. Just be sure to contact them well in advance.

WHERE TO GET INVOLVED

CLUBS AND SOCIETIES

ACE Races
www.aceraces.com
01952 249942

Dynamic Adventure Racing
www.dynamicadventureracing.com
01425 674 326

Questars
www.questars.co.uk
01380 831 388

Sleep Monsters
www.sleepmonsters.co.uk
01455 274691

13 BOULDERING

BUZZ FOR YOUR BUCK 7/10
THRILL FACTOR

'Bouldering is climbing in its most elemental form – the freedom of movement you get, whether indoors or out, is something more people could and should try.'

***Natalie Berry**, British Bouldering Champion 2005 and 2006*

Bouldering sounds more like a day out with Barney Rubble and Fred Flintstone than an adventure sport. Bouldering can involve – obviously – boulders, but it won't see you donning your leopard-skin tunic for a day out in Bedrock. Rather, bouldering is described by many as the purest form of climbing.

What sets bouldering apart from climbing is that no ropes or equipment are used. Given this lack of help, bouldering sensibly takes place at heights of generally no more than a few metres. However, less sensibly, you may find

BOULDERING: FOR PEOPLE WHO LIKE TO HANG OUT

yourself hanging upside down as you try and climb from the underside of an overhanging rock to the top (although, if it's any consolation, there'll probably be a crash mat underneath to protect you if you fall). Typically, bouldering is practised on large boulders, overhanging rocks, at the base of larger rock faces or climbing routes and even on man-made structures.

The route you take when you're bouldering is aptly referred to as the 'problem'. This stands to reason, since a climb is often purely about problem solving your way along the short and curious route. The focus in bouldering is always on the 'move' rather than endurance, so you'll see people practising the same 'problem' time and time again to get it right.

Originally invented as practice training for climbers, bouldering is now very much a sport in its own right. Today, many indoor climbing gyms have built bouldering areas and there are some entire gyms dedicated to the sport. Perhaps what keeps people coming back for more is that bouldering, with its long list of challenging, technical moves, isn't just about muscle – it's also about mental ability and often complex problem solving. Bridging, matching, rockover and undercling are just a selection of the moves and terms you'll want to get familiar with. And then you'll be ready to tackle the British Bouldering Championships, organised by the British Mountaineering Council.

GETTING STARTED

Bouldering is an easy sport to get involved with because it requires little or no equipment (most clubs or centres hire out footwear and chalk, used for grip). In theory, you can go out on your own and just start bouldering. However, we would recommend that you visit a climbing centre first, for a few lessons. Bouldering is a very social sport and can be done in big groups, so by going to a centre you'll meet like-minded people you can climb with. You'll need to be physically fit too, as bouldering requires a great deal of strength and power.

TAKING IT FURTHER

Apart from having fun doing it, you may want to take bouldering to the next level. As with climbing (see pages 80–85), there are grading systems for the sport, and this is where you can really start to push yourself. The V-grade system is one of the grading systems, with easier climbs graded V0; the scale continues to the current highest grade of V16. However, the grading system is an open-ended scale, so the world really is your oyster when it comes to bouldering.

WHERE TO GET INVOLVED

ADMINISTRATIVE BODIES

British Mountaineering Council (BMC)
www.thebmc.co.uk
0870 0104878

The British Mountaineering Council (BMC) is the representative body that exists to protect the freedoms and promote the interests of climbers, hill walkers and mountaineers. The BMC's website lists clubs across the UK, and the Regional Access Database will give you lots of information about your local crag, for example, access, birds nesting, etc.

Mountaineering Council of Scotland
www.mountaineering-scotland.org.uk
01738 493942

CLUBS AND SOCIETIES

Get in touch with a club near you and they'll be able to recommend the nearby climbing facilities that they use and where you'll be able to have lessons. Taking advice from experienced and enthusiastic climbers is vital and will be the best way to help you find a place to learn that's right for you.

You'll also find an area on the BMC website that allows you to search for local and national clubs. We've listed many of those clubs below.

South-east and London

Chelmsford Mountaineering Club
www.chelmsfordmountainclub.co.uk
enquiry@chelmsfordmountainclub.co.uk

Hertfordshire Mountaineering Club
www.thehmc.co.uk
chairman@thehmc.co.uk

Maidstone Mountaineering Club
www.mmce.co.uk

Marylebone Mountaineering Club
www.themmc.org.uk

Meadhurst Mountaineering Club
www.meadhurstmc.org.uk

Reading Mountaineering Club
www.readingmountaineeringclub.org.uk
01494 533828

Slough Mountaineering Club
www.slough-mountaineering.org.uk

Surbiton & Kingston Mt Club
www.sakmc.org
sakmc@hotmail.com

WHERE TO GET INVOLVED

South-west

Gloucestershire Mountaineering Club
www.thegmc.org.uk
MembershipSecretary@thegmc.org.uk

Wales and West Midlands

Clwyd Mountaineering Club
www.clwydmountaineeringclub.co.uk
01248 355985

Mercian Mountaineering Club
www.mercianmc.co.uk
07876 751557

Rugby Mountaineering Club
www.rugbymc.uklinux.net
01788 890777

Solihull Mountaineering Club
www.solihullmc.org.uk
membership@solihullmc.org.uk

East Midlands

Clogwyn Mountaineering Club
www.clogwyn.org.uk
01283 734126

Northern England

Carlisle Mountaineering Club
www.freetimeonline.co.uk/CMC/Index.cfm

Eden Valley Mountaineering Club
www.evmc.co.uk
01768 866082

Scotland

Braes O'Fife Mountaineering Club
www.braesofife.org.uk
01592 599051

Cairn Ban Mountaineering Club
www.acairnban.org.uk
07717 298556

14 CAVING

BUZZ FOR YOUR BUCK 8/10
THRILL FACTOR

How would you like to explore places where no human being has previously set foot? Do you want to participate in a sport that lets you escape to a world without mobile phones, cars or any other modern-world distractions? If so, caving could be for you. Entering a cave is like visiting an entirely different world, one that is exciting, unknown and definitely adrenaline-fuelled. The underground scenery can be spectacular, and the realisation that only a very few people have ever seen it before will leave you buzzing with excitement.

People have been exploring caves for thousands of years. Some cavers research living geology, survey and map underground, take photographs, or work in one of the many cave-related areas of science. Other cavers study bats, look for archaeological or paleaontological (fossil) sites, or study the hydrology of a region. Yet, it's only in the last century that caving has become a popular adventure sport.

There are a large number of different caves in the UK: horizontal, vertical, flooded, dry, cold, draughty, muddy and sandy. You'll need to learn and employ a multitude of techniques to explore them. You might use Single Rope Technique (SRT) to ascend and descend pitches (drops) in caves, or climbing (and crawling) techniques to find new passages within caves. In more advanced caving, you'll dig to find new, unexplored passages and you may well have to cave dive to pass through short, flooded sections of a cave. No caving trip will ever be the same, and it's perhaps this variety and the desire to chart new territory that keeps cavers coming back for more.

GETTING INVOLVED

Caving is absolutely not a sport to do on your own. It's all about team effort and support, and working with other, skilled cavers who know the areas you're exploring. The experience will be a physical and psychological test, with typical caving trips lasting about 6–10 hours, and long spells spent crawling along on your stomach under very low ceilings through slimy mud or cold water. And then there are your fellow cave-dwellers: bats, centipedes,

CAVING INCLUDES LONG PERIODS IN MUDDY WATER – THINK YOU CAN TAKE THE CHALLENGE?

spiders and all manner of other creepy crawlies, all to contend with in varying torchlight visibility. But if all this sounds like your perfect day out, then get yourself signed up to a caving club and begin exploring the wonders of the underground world.

As a beginner you'll need to become a member of a caving organisation. Most clubs organise trips for beginners, which will introduce you to the necessary caving skills and allow you to test out your endurance for small spaces and hard, physical effort. Caves can be dangerous, with hypothermia, falls, flooding and physical exhaustion a real risk, so it is vital you take part in this sport using the services of a *bona fide* club, society or organisation.

CAVING: CRAWLING THROUGH MUD IS ALL PART OF THE THRILL

EQUIPMENT NEEDED

The society, club or organisation you go caving with will provide all the necessary 'technical' equipment you need, such as ropes and ladders. Make sure you wear old and warm clothing (caves in the UK are a fairly constant temperature of about 8–10 °C/46–50 °F). Wear an old pair of boots such as army boots or Wellington boots (which most people use). Never wear trainers as they give no protection and little grip. It is a good idea to wear a boiler suit on top of your clothes (never let it be said that caving isn't stylish) as this stops your clothes moving around too much while you're crawling. Once you've been bitten by the caving bug (of the non-insect, cave-dwelling variety) you'll want to invest in a specialist suit and waterproof oversuit. A good helmet is a vital piece of kit; strap a small light on the front so your hands are free and you can see where you're going. Knee and elbow pads are useful for when you're crawling. And don't forget to wear a good pair of really hard-wearing gloves. If you're going on an all-day trip into the caves, you'll also need to plan to take food supplies, particularly water.

The list of caving equipment is longer than those for many other adventure sports, but while you may not be travelling at great speeds or falling from great heights, you are taking part in a risk-filled, exciting sport that may well see you going where no man has gone before. Enjoy the adventure.

WHERE TO GET INVOLVED

ADMINISTRATIVE BODIES

British Caving Association
www.british-caving.org.uk
01298 873 800

For the most comprehensive information on caving and details of all British Caving Association registered clubs, go to www.trycaving.co.uk.

This informative site that is the first point of call for anyone interested in caving.

15 CLIMBING AND ICE CLIMBING

BUZZ FOR YOUR BUCK 4/10
THRILL FACTOR ■■■□□□□□□□

Are you climbing the walls of your office and longing for another fix of adventure sports? Do your colleagues look at you strangely as you abseil back down to your desk? If you're hooked on climbing – and people who climb are – then the temptation to climb your office walls might not be so far from the truth. Climbing is a huge sport worldwide, and one taken very seriously in the UK.

If you've never climbed before, or perhaps haven't even considered doing it, there are two things worth thinking about. The first is that climbing is an excellent workout and is great for toning and building muscles (so no need for boring trips to the gym). The second is that you won't break the bank doing it. Learning to climb at an indoor centre is inexpensive, as is climbing outdoors. So this sport offers great exercise for little money. And that's before you've even considered the adrenaline rush you'll get from doing it. . .

There are many different disciplines and ways of climbing: indoor, traditional, bouldering (see also pages 70–75), sport, speed, free, solo, ice . . . and so the list goes on. Indoor climbing is the easiest one to start with as lots of centres offer classes in it. Once there, you can make the climb as hard or as easy as you want while you get to grips with the equipment and master belaying, abseiling, rope techniques and efficient movement. Once you're feeling confident on an indoor climbing wall, it's time to get outside and give outdoor climbing a go.

There are several types of outdoor sport climbing. These include the following:

- *Sport climbing* was developed in the 1980s and involves routes that have safety equipment, such as bolts, permanently fixed in the rock. Typically, this sort of climbing takes place in quarries and other designated areas, not mountain crags and sea cliffs.
- If you want to try crags and cliffs, then *traditional climbing*, in which you place removable equipment into whatever you're climbing up, might be your next step.
- *Speed climbing* is, as the name suggests, all about speed. The idea is to travel light and fast. Given the limited equipment you carry, this is dangerous and only for the seriously experienced climber.
- *Free climbers* risk life and limb as they scale the heights using only their hands, while *soloing* sees climbers going it alone. Both these disciplines are extremely dangerous and even the experts advise people against doing them – you've got no ropes, no company and no margin for error.

Ice climbing is, quite literally, the coolest climbing around. Imagine you're in a valley with deep snow covering the hillsides and roads. It's cold, the air is fresh, the sky is blue, your 'front points' are gripping the ice and your ice axes are in good placements. You can hear the trickle of the water deep down in the frozen waterfall that you're climbing. This is, quite simply, a great physical and emotional experience.

An offshoot of mountain climbing, ice climbing started in the nineteenth century when mountain climbers encountered the hard-water ice in the gullies and faces of the mountains they wanted to scale. Early mountain climbers, desperate to be the first to climb Mont Blanc, the Matterhorn and Mount Everest etc., but with only the most basic equipment, were forced to choose the easiest routes to reach the summit. For them, survival was a great achievement. As the sport of mountaineering matured and became more popular, climbers looked for other (often more difficult) routes to scale the mountains. This led climbers to train and practice techniques closer to home such as scaling cliffs, crags and gullies. Through the adoption of climbing techniques by mountaineers, rock and ice climbing became a sport in its own right.

Given the unpredictable nature of ice, ice climbing is a dangerous sport. You need to be a proficient general climber before you tackle ice climbing. You'll also need to be alert to the risks of avalanches, falling ice and ice that is too soft to provide secure protection for the ice screws, ice hooks and pound-ins. But when you're ready for the challenge, it'll be worth it. Climbing frozen waterfalls amid stunning scenery in sub-zero temperatures with the use of a couple of ice axes and some crampons is incredible – dangerous, but incredible.

Whatever climbing discipline you want to aim for, this sport is about physical strength, grace and the mental toughness needed to reach the top of whatever you've embarked on. These challenges, combined with the fact that climbing is a relatively inexpensive adventure sport, perhaps explain why so many people in the UK are addicted to climbing. So, next time you're scaling the walls of your office, remember that you could be on your way to a place in the Climbing World Cup – or for those of you with an environmental bent, how about trying the ISA International Tree Climbing Championships?

ICE CLIMBING CAN BE DANGEROUS, SO MAKE SURE YOU KEEP YOUR COOL.

GETTING INVOLVED

GETTING STARTED

Climbing clubs and indoor climbing walls are a great place to meet other climbers and to learn basic skills. Most club climbers can teach enough

TACKLING STEEP CLIMBS CAN BE MENTALLY AND PHYSICALLY CHALLENGING

rope techniques to keep you safe. While you're there, make sure you watch out for those climbers that move gracefully, which allows you to progress more efficiently and makes strenuous routes easier. Watching others climb will teach you a great deal.

Alternatively, go on a climbing course at one of the many outdoor centres or climbing walls that have sprung up near every major city, or book an individual lesson. Introductory courses at centres where there are indoor climbing walls are a very reasonable way to learn: expect to pay between £50 and £70 for a course offering two or three sessions. After that, using a climbing wall costs about £7 per session, plus hire for any equipment (boots and harness about £2.50 each). This sort of tuition will hopefully provide you with knowledge of the rope techniques that will help you avoid danger and awareness of how and when to apply them on a climb. Ultimately, however, all of this can only be learned with considerable climbing experience, so be prepared for a considerable time investment.

TAKING IT FURTHER

Once you feel proficient in rock climbing, are confident with the safety skills required, and have a large amount of experience under your belt, then you might want to hire an instructor to show you the basics of more demanding climbing, such as speed climbing or ice climbing.

EQUIPMENT NEEDED

Climbing centres and clubs will advise you on what kit you need and what kit they can hire out to you. Your requirements will depend on the type of climbing you want to do, but the bare essentials for rock climbing include: rock shoes, chalk bag, harness, helmet, belaying device, HMS screwgate, rope, karabiners, gloves and – most importantly – a thorough knowledge of how to use all the gear properly.

WHERE TO GET INVOLVED

ADMINISTRATIVE BODIES

British Mountaineering Council (BMC)
www.thebmc.co.uk
0870 0104878

The British Mountaineering Council (BMC) is the representative body that exists to protect the freedoms and promote the interests of climbers, hill walkers and mountaineers. The BMC's website lists clubs across the UK, and the Regional Access Database will give you lots of information about your local crag, for example, access, birds nesting, etc.

Mountaineering Council of Scotland
www.mountaineering-scotland.org.uk
01738 493942

CLUBS AND SOCIETIES

Get in touch with a club near you and they'll be able to recommend the nearby climbing facilities that they use and where you'll be able to have lessons. Taking advice from experienced and enthusiastic climbers is vital and will be the best way to help you find a place to learn that's right for you.

You'll also find an area on the BMC website that allows you to search for local and national clubs. We've listed many of those clubs below.

South-east and London

Cambridge Climbing and Caving Club
www.thecccc.org.uk.uk
mebership@thecccc.org.uk

Chelmsford Mountaineering Club
www.chelmsfordmountainclub.co.uk
enquiry@chelmsfordmountainclub.co.uk

WHERE TO GET INVOLVED

Hertfordshire Mountaineering Club
www.thehmc.co.uk
chairman@thehmc.co.uk

Maidstone Mountaineering Club
www.mmce.co.uk

Marylebone Mountaineering Club
www.themmc.org.uk

Meadhurst Mountaineering Club
www.meadhurstmc.org.uk

Slough Mountaineering Club
www.slough-mountaineering.org.uk

Surbiton & Kingston Mt Club
www.sakmc.org
sakmc@hotmail.com

South-west

Gloucestershire Mountaineering Club
www.thegmc.org.uk
MembershipSecretary@thegmc.org.uk

Wessex Mountaineering Club
www.wessexmc.org.uk
secretary@wessexmc.org.uk

Wales and West Midlands

Clwyd Mountaineering Club
www.clwydmountaineeringclub.co.uk
01248 355985

Gwent Mountaineering Club
www.gwentmountaineeringclub.
org.uk
02920 852771

Mercian Mountaineering Club
www.mercianmc.co.uk
07876 751557

Rugby Mountaineering Club
www.rugbymc.uklinux.net
01788 890777

Solihull Mountaineering Club
www.solihullmc.org.uk
membership@solihullmc.org.uk

Pembrokeshire Activity Centre
www.pembrokeshire-activity-
centre.co.uk

East Midlands

Clogwyn Mountaineering Club
www.clogwyn.org.uk
01283 734126

Oread Mountaineering Club
www.oread.co.uk

Northern England

Carlisle Mountaineering Club
www.freetimeonline.co.uk/CMC/Index
.cfm

Eden Valley Mountaineering Club
www.evmc.co.uk
01768 866082

Scotland

Braes O'Fife Mountaineering Club
www.braesofife.org.uk
01592 599051

Cairn Ban Mountaineering Club
www.cairnban.org.uk
07717 298556

Perth Mountaineering Club
www.perthmountaineering-club.co.uk
01561 340673

LAND

16 KARTING

BUZZ FOR YOUR BUCK 7/10
THRILL FACTOR

'Words can't describe the buzz you get from karting. As a sixteen-year-old competing in some of the top races in the UK, I just wish I'd started when I was even younger – well, when you're driving round a course at 80 mph, just inches off the ground, who wouldn't?'

Michael Comber*, 2006 TKM Festival Champion, Super One Champion and British TKM Champion*

Is karting every boy-racer's dream? Undoubtedly. No matter whether you're ten, twenty or twice that age, karting (or go-karting as some people call it) still has huge appeal as it allows anyone the opportunity to get out on the track for a day of high-speed, corner-gripping, rubber-burning fun.

Karts are small, four-wheeled vehicles also known as go-karts or gearbox/shifter karts, depending on the design. A kart must have no suspension (trust me, mine didn't) and no differential (i.e. solid back axle); they are usually raced on a scaled-down track. Karting isn't just a fun day out, it can also be an important, safer and less expensive stepping stone into the higher and more expensive ranks of motor racing. In fact, many Formula One racers grew up racing karts – Michael Schumacher and Ayrton Senna, for example, both took this route. Norfolk-living Oliver Oakes, having won nearly every karting title there is, took to the winner's podium as Karting World Champion in 2005 before going on to Formula BMW racing. What kart racing does is help drivers develop quick reflexes, precision control and decision-making skills, all vital if you want to go further in racing . . . and if we were betting people here at Ride of My Life, we would be putting some money on the future of sixteen-year-old karter Michael Comber from Leicestershire.

Karts vary in speed and some can reach speeds of over 255 km/h (160 mph). A kart with a 100cc two-stroke engine can accelerate from 0–97 km/h (0–60 mph) in under 4 seconds (depending on the weight of the driver) and has a top speed of 120 km/h (75 mph). You can expect your heart rate to be pounding through the roof while you're tearing round a track at these sorts of speeds so low to the ground. . .

At the end of a day's karting at a track near you, don't let the fun stop – why not set your sights on taking it further and getting involved in club racing? Who knows, one day you could be competing at national or even international events. And whether you call it karting or go-karting, you'll have the ride of your life!

KARTING: BEING DRIVEN ROUND THE BEND WAS NEVER SO MUCH FUN!

GETTING INVOLVED

Due to the large number of kart circuits around the UK, it's easy to try karting. If this experience leaves you wanting more – and we'll bet our overdrafts it will – then take a test day in a two-stroke kart. However, kart circuits won't offer you the use of competition-level karts, so the next best step is to investigate the twenty or so kart classes in the UK and join a local club. Clubs hold meetings for most classes on a regular basis.

TAKING IT FURTHER

If you want to take karting further, it's time to set your sights on clambering on to a podium and get involved in racing. Typically, race formats will be either sprint or endurance. As the names suggest, the sprint format is about speed and is a series of short-duration races, normally for a small number of laps that qualify for a final. There will be different point-scoring calculations that determine the event's overall winner. These races tend to last no longer than 15 minutes; as the driver you'll be focusing on speed and passing other drivers. Endurance races are about just that – endurance. You might be racing for anything from 30 minutes to 24 hours; in these races your focus will be on consistency, reliability and pit strategy.

GREAT BRITAIN'S MICHAEL COMBER IN ACTION (CENTRE)

EQUIPMENT NEEDED

We don't recommend you embark on buying a kart until you've done a lot of research. Visit a couple of local clubs and talk to the drivers and mechanics. You might find someone who is about to upgrade their kart and is willing to give you a practice day on the one they are looking to sell.

By joining a club you will get access to the local kart traders and they will help you make the decision about which class and equipment is best for you. It is not necessary to go out and buy a brand new kart (which could cost you upwards of £3000) as there is a good second-hand market. But, again, ensure you do your research and only by a kart you have tested or seen race. Expect to pay £1000 plus for a reasonable second-hand 'starter' kart. You will also need to purchase suitable protective clothing, which includes approved crash helmet (allow £150), racing suit (£100), gloves (£25) and boots (£25).

WHERE TO GET INVOLVED

ADMINISTRATIVE BODIES

National Karting Association
www.nationalkarting.co.uk
01203 322 726

North of Ireland Karting Association
www.nikarting.com
07779 115 414

Scottish Karting Club
www.scottishkarting.co.uk
01698 886 201

CLUBS AND COMPANIES

South-east and London

Bayford Meadows Kart Circuit
www.bayfordkarting.co.uk
01795 410 707

Brentwood Park Karting
www.brentwood-karting.com
01277 260 001

Buckmore Park Karting Ltd
www.buckmore.co.uk
01634 201 562

Lakeside Karting
www.lakeside-karting.com
01708 863070

Lydd International Raceway at Herons Park
www.heronspark.com
01797 321 895

Playscape Pro-Racing Ltd
www.playscape.co.uk
020 8677 8494

Q Leisure
www.qleisure.co.uk
01273 834 403

WHERE TO GET INVOLVED

The Raceway Kings X
www.theraceway.net
020 7833 1000

Rayleigh Karting
www.essexkarting.co.uk
01268 777 765

Revolution Karting
www.revolutionkarting.com
020 7538 5195

Teamsport Indoor Karting – Camberley, Crawley, Gosport
www.team-sport.co.uk
0870 6000 601

South-west

Drive Tech Ltd
www.combe-events.co.uk
01249 783 010

JDR Karting
www.indoorkartingcentre.com
01452 311 211

Minimoto Racing Ltd
www.minimoto.co.uk
01666 838 234

The Raceway Bristol
www.theraceway.co.uk
0800 376 6111

Teamsport Indoor Karting
www.team-sport.co.uk
0870 6000 601

Teamsport Indoor Karting – Andover
www.team-sport.co.uk
0870 6000 601

Teamsport Indoor Karting – Southampton
www.team-sport.co.uk
0870 6000 601

Wales and West Midlands

BP Karting
www.bpkarting.com
01437 769 555

Cannon Raceway
www.cannonraceway.co.uk
01902 565 000

Crazy Karting
www.crazykarting.co.uk
01952 588885

Fast Lane Karting
www.fastlanekarting.co.uk
01782 250 450

Herefordshire Raceway
www.herefordshireraceway.org.uk
01544 318 334

Priory Park Circuit
www.priorypark.co.uk
01827 899 800

The Raceway Birmingham
www.theraceway.co.uk
0800 376 6111

SupaKart
www.supakart.co.uk
01633 280 808

Teamworks Karting Ltd
www.teamworkskarting.com
0870 900 3020

Teamsport Indoor Karting – Cardiff
www.team-sport.co.uk
0870 6000 601

WHERE TO GET INVOLVED

East Midlands

Amen Corner Karting
www.amencornerkarting.co.uk
01623 822 205

Langer Kart & Quad Centre
www.lkqc.com
01949 861 155

Nottingham Raceway
www.nottinghamracewaykarting.co.uk
01664 822 750

Stretton 2000 Ltd
www.stretton2000.com
0116 259 2900

East of England

Anglia Indoor Kart Racing Ltd
www.angliakarting.com
01473 240087

Karttrak
www.karttrak.co.uk
01263 512 649

Northern England

Karting North East
www.kartingnortheast.co.uk
0191 521 4050

Mersey Indoor Karting
www.merseykarting.co.uk
0151 734 1736

Raceway Karting
www.racewaykarting.co.uk
01924 477 000

Speedkarting Ltd
www.speedkarting.co.uk
01925 415 114

Trax Motorsport Ltd
www.traxmotorsport.co.uk
01772 731 832

West Coast Indoor Karting
www.westcoastkarting.co.uk
01900 816 472

Scotland

Dumfries Speedkart Ltd
www.dumfries-speedkart.co.uk
01387 721 111

Knockhill Racing Circuit
www.knockhillkarting.co.uk
01383 626 264

Raceland
www.raceland.co.uk
0131 665 6525

Racing Karts
www.racingkarts.co.uk
01506 410 123

ScotKart Indoor Kart Racing
www.scotkart.co.uk
0141 641 0222

Xtreme Karting
www.xtremekarting.co.uk
01324 579 797

Northern Ireland

Formula Karting Racing
www.formula-karting.com
028 302 66 220

Speedway Karting Ltd
www.speedwaykarting.com
028 93342777

17

KITE LANDBOARDING, KITE BUGGYING, BUGGY JUMPING

BUZZ FOR YOUR BUCK 8/10
THRILL FACTOR

Kites, cameras, action – oh, and wind, but not necessarily too much. . . The popularity of kite sports shows no signs of abating; in fact, quite the reverse. With more new kite sports coming to UK shores, if you haven't tried one yet, now's the time to get on board . . . specifically a land board or buggy.

KITE LANDBOARDING

Based on the popular kite surfing (see pages 156–160), kite landboarding involves riders hitting large empty areas, such as hard-packed sandy beaches, tarmac or grass, with mountainboards or landboards and a large kite attached to a harness. But this sport is not just about ripping along the beach at high speeds. Rather, the emphasis for competent riders is freestyle manoeuvres using the kite to pull them into the air and perform tricks such as flips, rotations and grabs. Some riders use ramps and other obstacles to perform tricks, reflecting the influence of skateboarding on the sport.

KITE LANDBOARDING: WHAT BETTER WAY TO FLY A KITE ON THE BEACH?

As with kite surfing, kite landboarding isn't for the faint-hearted. While it isn't all about strength, you need to be coordinated, relatively fearless and prepared for a few falls and scrapes along the way.

GETTING STARTED

There are commercial companies that run both taster courses for the absolute beginner and courses to take you to the next stage. Once you've put some serious time in on the sand, grass or tarmac and want to progress to an advanced level, one-to-one training will help you pull some serious stunts . . . and send your street cred intergalactic.

EQUIPMENT NEEDED

Other than the kite and the board, the key piece of equipment you need for this sport is a helmet – kite landboarding involves speed and high lifts off the ground, so protecting your head is essential. Padding, such as knee and shoulder pads, is also recommended for protection in the event of falls.

The actual kite is a large sail (these vary in size according to wind conditions) usually made of strong rip-stop nylon. They can be flown with two, four or five lines. You control the kite using a control bar or set of handles.

Boards vary hugely, being made from wood or lighter, composite materials. The size of boards also differs. Beginners might choose a larger board for added stability, while more experienced riders who want to perform tricks tend to opt for smaller, lighter boards. As with kite surfing, all boards have foot bindings.

In addition to a harness, you'll probably also want to buy a ground stake, to hold the kite down when it's landed, and a wind meter.

The equipment list for kite landboarding isn't short or inexpensive, so take plenty of advice from the experts when you're looking to buy. Best of all, join a club where fellow members can give impartial advice and help with what to choose. Clubs may also be able to help you source good, second-hand equipment.

KITE BUGGYING AND BUGGY JUMPING

Kite buggying is a relative newcomer to the adventure sports scene but is already proving a popular form of power kiting, as it's easy to learn and relatively safe. Developed in the early 1990s by Peter Lynn in New Zealand, kite buggies are classified as Class 8 Land Yachts. The buggy in which you sit is a light, single-seated, stainless steel vehicle. With one front wheel (which you steer with your feet) and two fixed back wheels, these buggies can easily achieve speeds of 48 km/h (30 mph); experienced drivers can reach speeds of up to 115 km/h (70 mph).

Unlike kite landboarding, where (typically) the kite is attached to you by a harness, the driver of a kite buggy holds the kite lines, giving optimum efficiency. When you start out you'll use a smaller kite and need to be confident in handling it without the buggy. Once you feel confident, position the kite overhead, leap into the buggy and get going! Experienced kite buggyers will be aiming to perform wheelies, power slides and reverse moves and spins, before letting the kite pull them into the air to perform 360-degree stunts. That's buggy jumping! Serious riders will be looking to stay airborne and perform awe-inspiring 720-degree buggy jumping stunts.

GETTING STARTED

It's easy to get started with kite buggying – with as little as 1.8 knots (5 mph) of wind, you will be buggying (although the lower the wind speed, the larger the kite you'll need). Clubs and societies across the UK offer courses for beginners which cover safety, power kite and buggy skills, and give you time to put the theory into practice.

Remember that for both kite landboarding and kite buggying, one of the challenges is being able to multi-task well. Looking upwards, you'll need to have one eye on the kite you're flying and controlling, but looking down, you'll need to have one eye on the ground, watching where your buggy's heading. Get both of these right and you'll be flying; get one wrong and . . . crash, bang, wallop!

TAKING IT FURTHER

Once you've done a beginner's course or feel competent handling your kite and buggy, many clubs and companies offer more advanced courses. These will cover coping with larger kites and more power, and will teach you freestyle tricks such as power slides, wheelies, reverse moves and spins. Alternatively, if you try freestyle but fancy something a bit faster then you may decide to do buggy racing. As the name suggests, buggy racing is all about going as fast as you can and faster than the other buggy pilots you are racing against.

EQUIPMENT NEEDED

Clubs and centres that run beginners' courses will hire out equipment when you're starting out. But given that you'll probably be bitten by the buggying bug, you may well want to go on and buy your own kit. You'll be looking to buy a buggy (expect to pay £220 plus for a new one), a kite (£100 plus for a beginners' kite. Allow more for lines, control bars etc.) and helmet (£20 plus). Clubs are a good place to research what second-hand equipment is available; otherwise there are plenty of companies who sell a wide range of new equipment. There's a (bafflingly) wide range of kites to choose from – two-line and four-line parafoils, stacked Flexifoils, stacked wings, single wings and so on. . . Take plenty of advice from the experts and don't rush into an expensive purchase.

WHERE TO GET INVOLVED

ADMINISTRATIVE BODIES

British Power Kitesports Association (BPKA)
www.bpka.co.uk
The BPKA is the largest independent power kiting club in the world, with over 4000 members who participate in kite sports such as kite landboarding and kite buggying (the organisation also covers kite surfing, kite skiing and power kiting).

To find your nearest club, society or meeting point for kite landboarders, check out the BPKA website for an up-to-date list. There is not a huge number of clubs specifically set up for kite landboarding – it is, after all, a relatively new sport. You will find that many of the clubs and centres that offer kite surfing will also offer kite landboarding and kite buggying, as will many of those clubs which list themselves simply as 'kite clubs'. Most kite landboarders and kite buggyers will be members of the BPKA first, so this makes the organisation an excellent starting point.

18

LAND YACHTING

BUZZ FOR YOUR BUCK 6/10
THRILL FACTOR ■■■■■■■□□□

'Sailing a land yacht gives you a buzz every time you accelerate away downwind with the windward wheel in the air and the ground rushing past beneath you, or drift sideways through a fast turn. All that speed, all that G-force, and all from the power of the wind.'

***Chris Wright**, Former World and British Land Yachting Champion*

Land sailing – isn't that a contradiction in terms? Luckily for us adventure-sport-loving lot, no. Land yachting, or land sailing, can trace its heritage back to Ancient Egypt, when craft were apparently built for leisure. It wasn't until 1909 that France and Belgium held the first beach-based races. At the same time, in the United States and Australia, land yachts were functional craft used to transport goods across dry lakes. Today, land yachting is a sport that's taken very seriously. Well, when you're travelling at speeds of up to 160 km/h (100 mph), who wouldn't be serious about land yachting?

Land yachts consist of a sail attached to a glass-fibre body and metal chassis. They work along similar principles to traditional sailing, apart from the fact that the pilot sits – in a near-lying position – in a body that has one wheel at the front, two at the back and no brakes (which is why, when travelling at speeds of up to 161 km/h (100 mph), this really is an 'adventure' sport!).

Racing is, unsurprisingly, a very competitive business. The International Land and Sand Yachting Federation (FISLY) presides over the racing rules. The World Championships take place every 2 years, but closer to home you will be able to participate in various local races and competitions throughout the year.

The classes of racing yacht are as follows:

- Class 3 yachts, with a maximum sail area of 7.35 sq m (80 sq ft), are the largest and most competitive land yachts, and arguably the fastest. They are also the most expensive: a new one could set you back up to £4000 plus.
- Class 5 yachts, although slower than Class 3, are one of the most popular classes. Reaching speeds of up to 112 k/ph (70 mph), Class 5 is so called because of the 5.5 sq m (59 sq ft) sails that are used. These yachts are ideal for novice and intermediate levels.
- Class 8 yachts are also known as parakarts and kite buggies (see pages 94–95). The sails are replaced with traction kites, which vary in size according to wind conditions. This class allows for freestyle riding and racing and is very popular due to the light-weight portability of the yachts
- Class 6 and mini-yachts, while not a formal class, are fun and informal racers. They use a windsurfer rig, while allowing the user to sit. Simply constructed, they are very easy to pack into the back of a car and make a great introduction to land yachting.

If you love speed and want the speed of motor racing with the grace of sailing, then land yachting could be for you. The Land Yacht World Speed Record currently stands at just over 187 km/h (116 mph), and even at low wind speeds, a racing yacht can easily travel at about 69 km/h (43 mph). This is amazing when you consider that hurtling along a deserted beach in this way, a few inches off the ground, is powered by nothing more than the wind.

GETTING INVOLVED

GETTING STARTED

There are plenty of opportunities around the UK for you to experience an introduction to land yachting. A 2- or 3-hour session will include a safety briefing, tuition and plenty of time for you to have a go. Some clubs and societies offer these taster sessions and commercial companies offer land yachting 'experiences.' Expect to pay around £50–£60 for a 3-hour session.

LAND YACHTING AT THE BRITISH CHAMPIONSHIPS, LYTHAM ST ANNES

TAKING IT FURTHER

Whether you're a beginner or want to take it further and learn to race competitively, many clubs and societies run training that will be suitable and is overseen by the British Federation of Sand and Land Yacht Clubs (BFSLYC). Learning to race through one of these clubs is a great way to meet other experienced enthusiasts, share the learning process and take advice. You will also be able to take part in club races and, should you get really good, start training for the World Championships.

EQUIPMENT NEEDED

For taster days and as a beginner, you will be able to hire all the equipment you need. Simply turn up dressed sensibly, with good footwear and possible wet weather gear (depending on the time of year and weather conditions.) As you progress, you may want to buy your own land yacht and sail. If you're a member of a land yachting club, this will be the best place to look for second-hand land yachts; it will also give you the opportunity to talk to other members about what and where you should buy. Costs depend on the class of yacht, but expect to pay between £600–£1000 for a new 'starter' yacht; and between £200–£600 for a second-hand one.

WHERE TO GET INVOLVED

ADMINISTRATIVE BODIES

The British Federation of Sand and Land Yacht Clubs
www.bfslyc.org.uk

International Land and Sand Yachting Federation
www.fisly.org
secretary@fisly.org.uk

Clubs and societies

South-east and London
Kirrawee Land Yachting
www.kirrawee.com
01797 362 132

Wales and West Midlands

Carmarthenshire Land Sailing
www.clsc.uk.net
ian@clsc.uk.net

East of England

The Anglia Land Yacht Club
www.anglialandsailing.co.uk
contact@anglialandsailing.co.uk

19 MOUNTAIN BIKING

BUZZ FOR YOUR BUCK 9/10
THRILL FACTOR

Were you Chopper and BMX mad? Well if so, you're probably going to be mountain bike mad, too. Mountain biking is a bit like grown-up BMXing – it's for people who love the buzz, adrenaline and speed they can get with pedal power. Mountain biking is a form of off-road cycling, using very sturdy bicycles with (usually) straight handlebars and wide tyres.

Mountain biking falls into two categories: downhill and cross-country. Mountain bikes used for downhill riding are usually full-suspension bicycles, with front and rear shock absorbers and disc brakes. Cross-country bikes are lighter in weight and typically have a front shock absorber, but none in the rear (although full-suspension bikes that are light enough for cross-country riding have recently been developed and are on the market). Unfortunately, whichever type of bike you buy, they're usually the type that thieves are rather partial to, particularly in cities. Ensure you keep your pride and joy well-secured and, if possible, out of sight when it's not in use.

There's nothing more complicated about mountain biking than riding a great bike on some great rides. There are bike trails all around the country, so you can choose one to suit your nerve. Once you've been biking for a while and have a good level of fitness, the next step is to try a race. You don't need to have a titanium bike and be carrying less fat on you than a butcher's pencil, or be Brad Pitt's stunt bottom (though that may help win you serious crowd support). All you need is a desire to see how well you can do and to push your fitness and riding skills to the limit. Novice races are a good way to start and they tend to have shorter technical sections, while the rest of the race is easier but instead places demands on your fitness. Most courses consist of a lap of several miles with three or four laps, taking between 1 and 2 hours to complete. Races are held for all age groups and levels.

GETTING INVOLVED

Mountain biking is one of the easiest adventure sports to become involved in because it's so accessible. Most of us are never too far from the countryside

MOUNTAIN BIKING: NOT FOR THE FAINT-HEARTED

where there are plenty of off-road routes and forestry trails. From a financial perspective, a good quality bike can be purchased for a few hundred pounds. Compared to other sports, mountain biking offers plenty of 'Buzz for Your Buck'.

Just taking your mountain bike out on a dirt road helps you get used to the bumps and the inconsistencies in the road, riding loosely, reading the road and looking ahead. That's really all you need to do, just get used to the feel of the bike over varied and uneven terrain. If you start out on trails that are too advanced or technically difficult, it'll be frustrating. Recreational or multi-use trails provide very even surfaces with a shallow grade. Practice on those, and from there you can move on.

EQUIPMENT NEEDED

Basic gear and equipment can be bought at reasonable prices. However if you fancy an ultra lightweight bike in carbon fibre with a sophisticated programmable suspension, you may need to start buttering up your bank manager, as these bikes can cost thousands of pounds. But avoid the cheaper-priced bikes because they are 'built to a price' and may not be strong enough to withstand proper off-road riding. You can get a good bike from a reputable manufacturer for about £300.

GETTING USED TO THE DIFFERENT TYPES OF TERRAIN IS ALL PART OF THE FUN OF MOUNTAIN BIKING!

The next most important piece of equipment is a good quality helmet. You'll also need cycling shorts or trousers with padding, which will allow you to ride for longer. Gloves will help reduce some of the vibrations that can cause blisters and they will also protect your hands if you fall. There is a wide range of mountain bike shoes on offer, some clip into the bike pedals while others look like traditional shoes but have rigid soles. Glasses will be a good investment as they offer you much needed protection from branches and flying dirt and mud – but ensure you go for quality and fit, not fashion. Finally, mud is the mainstay of mountain biking, and the wetter the better. So make sure you've got a waterproof jacket and trousers and a long sleeve shirt in breathable fabric.

WHERE TO GET INVOLVED

ADMINISTRATIVE BODIES

International Mountain Biking Association UK (IMBA)
www.imba-uk.com

The IMBA promotes mountain biking in the UK and Ireland, defends rights of way, supports environmentally sound and socially responsible mountain biking, and works to keep trails and public access open for mountain biking by encouraging responsible riding and supporting volunteer trail work.

British Cycling
www.britishcycling.org.uk
0870 871 2000

British Cycling is the internationally recognised governing body of cycling in the UK. It administers the sport in the following disciplines: BMX, Cycle Speedway, Cyclo-Cross, Mountain Bike, Road and Track.

North Wales Mountain Biking Association
www.nwmba.org.uk

The association is affiliated, through the Welsh Cycling Union, with British Cycling. It has organised racing at local and regional level, as well as hosting a number of national events in the disciplines of Cross Country, Hillclimb, Downhill and Trials, including National Points and National Championships.

Clubs and societies

There are a wealth of active and very enthusiastic mountain biking clubs and societies throughout the UK, enough to write a separate book about. So, rather than give you a list that unfairly includes just a smattering of all these great clubs and misses out many, we're going to refer you to the excellent website of British Cycling (www.britishcycling.org.uk), where you'll find more clubs listed than I've had punctures (and that's saying something). Many of the clubs have websites, and you'll be spoiled for choice as to where you can go and cycle to your heart's content.

20 MOUNTAIN BOARDING

BUZZ FOR YOUR BUCK 10/10
THRILL FACTOR ■■■■■□□□□□

I suspect we all secretly (and not so secretly) love tobogganing. But dreams of winter days spent screaming with excitement, as we fly down snow-covered hills, remain just that – dreams. The UK's feeble attempt at snow means that in most parts of the country we're left miserably shuffling our rarely used toboggans over tufts of grass and patchy, soggy snow. However all is not lost. There's an adventure sport out there that will once more see you hurtling down hills and grinning from ear to ear: mountain boarding.

Mountain boarding, or All Terrain Boarding (ATB), is a relatively new summer sport that has derived from snowboarding. Originally invented by keen snowboarders who still wanted to be able to practise their skills when there was no snow on the ground, the popularity of mountain boarding means that it is now very much a sport in its own right, and no longer the poor relation of snowboarding.

In fact, the UK has become the mountain boarding centre of the world. Britain's rolling hills provide the ideal terrain for the many mountain board parks that have sprung up around the country and even some clever, cash-strapped farmers have diversified and made their land available for mountain boarding.

Mountain boarding is a relatively easy and cheap sport to start taking part in. You can hire your equipment by the hour at a mountain boarding centre and after a few hours you'll be on your way; from learning the tricks of the trade to hurtling down a mountain at up to 80.4 k/ph (50 mph).

WORK YOUR WAY UP TO TRICKS AND JUMPS

A mountain board is similar to an oversized skateboard, but with much larger wheels and normally two-foot bindings. Wheel sizes vary and will depend on which of the three categories of mountain boarding you're taking part in: downhill (riding on a pre-designed track), freestyle (doing tricks and jumps) or free riding (just hurtling down a hill as fast as your wheels will carry you). The fancier the ride, the smaller the wheel. The faster the ride, the fatter the wheel.

When you've mastered the basics and want to push yourself to the next stage, why not work towards competing in some of the competitions and races held all around the country? Before long you'll be racing slalom, battling it out with your opponent as you weave between poles, jump, carve down hills and have the time of your life. Then go into the pub and tell your mates about power-slides, jumpstarting, tabletops, step-ups, back flips, front flips, board grabs and rollers. "You did all that on an old sheep farm in Wales?" they'll ask in disbelief.

GETTING INVOLVED

An hour long beginners' lesson at one of the many centres around the UK will get you started – in fact beginner lessons are mandatory at many centres – and you'll be surprised at how quickly you will get going. Importantly, a lesson will teach you the basics of stopping safely and controlling speed, rather than learning the painful way. Get the bug – and we're pretty sure you will – and most centres will offer improvement or private lessons to ensure you keep progressing. Then you can set your sights on the excitement of the All Terrain Boarding World Series. Expect to pay from about £12–16 for an hour's lesson and equipment hire, or £7–12 just to hire the equipment.

EQUIPMENT NEEDED

A board, helmet, knee pads, elbow pads and wrist supports are all your essentials and you can hire these from the centres until you're ready to buy your own. Wear sports footwear, or if you have any ankle problems or weaknesses, footwear that offers ankle support.

WHERE TO GET INVOLVED

ADMINISTRATIVE BODIES

All Terrain Boarding Association UK (ATBA-UK)
www.atbauk.org
0870 765 8240

ATBA-UK is a non-profit-making organisation and the recognised forum for mountain boarding in the UK. It aims to promote the sport by putting riders' interests first, promoting safety, sanctioning events and providing training.

CLUBS, SOCIETIES AND COMPANIES

There are many, many clubs and commercial companies for this exciting sport . . . and the list will continue to grow! We've listed some of them here for you.

South-east and London

Hare Down ATB
www.haredown.com
0124 381 1976

South-west

Extreme Academy
www.extremeacademy.co.uk
01637 860 840

Ivy Leaf Mountain Board Centre
www.ivyleafmountainboarding.co.uk
07773 069716

South-west Mountain Board Centre
www.sw-mbc.co.uk
07866 398 599

Wales and West Midlands

ATB Wales
www.atb-wales.co.uk

Bugs Boarding
www.bugsboarding.co.uk
07749 897 330

Out to Grass
www.outtograss.com
01886 880 099

Ride the Hill
www.ridethehill.com
01453 519 113

Northern England

Another World Mountain Boarding Centre
www.mountainboarding.co.uk
01422 245196

Surf the Turf
www.surf-the-turf.co.uk
07740 861 019

Scotland

Arran Adventure Company
www.arranadventure.com
01770 302

Bennachie Mountainboard Centre
www.scottish-boarding.com
07766 817 478

21 PARKOUR AND FREE RUNNING

OFF THE RATINGS!

Forget getting to work on the crowded bus or by train, forget being stuck in rush hour traffic or trudging the pavements alongside the hundreds of other commuters as they make their way unwillingly to work. Why not jump over rooftops, leap buildings, scale walls and arrive at your desk with a well-rehearsed routine of a flip and a roll? (Just avoid picking up a takeaway coffee on the way in.)

It was a Frenchman who came up with the idea of parkour and Sebastien Foucan, one of the pioneers of the sport, then went on to develop free running out of this. The idea of parkour is that you pass obstacles (on foot) in the fastest and most direct manner possible. So if you're running along and there's a wall in your path, you don't go out of your way to find a route around it, you move over it. So parkour involves jumping, vaulting, rolling, flipping and climbing to move over objects in an uninterrupted way.

Parkour and free running are similar beasts in many ways and share some of the same techniques, but free running focuses on the aesthetics of the sport. A more creative way of running and with more scope for personal interpretation, free running isn't so much about how fast you get somewhere, but how you look getting there. Elegance, fluidity and the use of 'tricks' all make you a better free runner.

Both sports are suited naturally to an urban environment where walls, rails, buildings and general concrete objects make up the landscape – as a free runner or traceur (someone who practises parkour) the city really is your playground. But parkour and free running are more than a sport: they are a way of living due to the training and focus that's needed to do either successfully, the dangers involved and the strong philosophies attached to them – think 'Spiderman-does-yoga'.

PARKOUR ACROBATS 3RUN DEMONSTRATE THEIR MOVES IN EAST LONDON

Learning to flow like water over 15-metre (50-foot) spiked railings isn't something you can pick up on a Saturday afternoon, so if you want to participate in these sports, you'll need to be prepared to invest the time. But if you do, it'll be much more than just an adrenaline rush you get from it; you'll be on your way to an inner balance, better fitness and a fascinating evolution of the mind.

So next time you're walking out of your front door and stumble over the dustbin that someone's left in the middle of the path, see it as an exciting opportunity to show your athletic aesthetics and leap over it . . . as gracefully as you can, of course.

GETTING INVOLVED

We don't need to tell you that parkour and free running are potentially very dangerous sports, so when starting you should take plenty of advice from people who are very experienced and allow them to train you. The best way to find experienced enthusiasts who can teach you is to go online and search sites such as the UK Parkour Association at www.parkour.org.uk. Active online forums give you the chance to ask advice from people with all levels of experience, discover how they got started and find people who you can meet up with to learn.

There are clubs springing up around the country, many of which were formed from the numerous online parkour and free-running communities.

EQUIPMENT NEEDED

The equipment list is small for both sports: comfortable running shoes and clothing that doesn't restrict or impinge on your movement (you may also want gloves to help give you grip). However, what you will also need to develop is strength, elasticity and an excellent level of fitness.

WHERE TO GET INVOLVED

CLUBS AND SOCIETIES

Parkour and free running are all about freedom and expressing individuality so it would seem counterintuitive to have pages of clubs here with endless committee members, forms to fill in and rules to abide by. However, there are groups of people who meet, online communities and networks. We're giving you a list here of excellent starting points and information resources:

Edinburgh Parkour
www.ed-pk.com

Glasgow Parkour
www.glasgowparkour.co.uk

Parkour World Association
www.pawa.ru

South Coast Parkour
www.scpk.info

UK Parkour Association
www.parkour.org.uk

Urban Freeflow
www.urbanfreeflow.com

22
QUAD BIKING

LAND

BUZZ FOR YOUR BUCK 4/10
THRILL FACTOR ■■■■□□□□□□

Farmers herd sheep with them, celebrities race around their estates on them (Posh and Becks have been photographed several times on theirs at Beckingham Palace) and lawyers race accountants on them. Quad bikes can be functional, they can be status symbols and they can offer great corporate days out. But what they offer most is fun.

Quad bikes, or all-terrain vehicles, were originally designed for farmers, shepherds and landowners who needed to cover distances too great and varying to do so easily on foot. But, luckily for us, some bright spark obviously spotted that quad bikes could be used for entertainment and adventure, too. As a result, quad biking centres and places offering quad biking experiences have sprung up all over the UK. The versatility of these 4-wheel drive vehicles means that centres are able to offer all sorts of terrains and activities: off-road tracks, quad trekking, race circuits, slalom courses, obstacle courses and staged competitions. They also offer a variety of vehicles suited to different ages and abilities, so you could be riding anything from a 125cc automatic quad, or a farm-style utility vehicle to one of the latest Suzuki sports bikes.

Now you may not think that quad biking is an adventure sport, but we'd disagree. When you're tearing around a track experiencing the ultimate in off-road racing, tearing down valleys, splashing through streams, negotiating your way through difficult terrain and getting covered in mud, try telling us your heart's not racing and you're not really having the time of your life. . .

QUAD BIKING: THE ULTIMATE IN FARM MACHINERY!

GETTING INVOLVED

Easy. Book a session and head down to a centre near you that offers quad biking. You'll be given a safety briefing and instruction session and then you'll be off. It really is that simple.

EQUIPMENT NEEDED

Centres will provide you with the essential equipment of crash helmets. They may well also provide boots, goggles and, if necessary, waterproof trousers. You just need to turn up in clothes you don't mind getting dirty and wet.

WHERE TO GET INVOLVED

CLUBS, SOCIETIES AND COMPANIES

South-east and London

Quad Safari
www.quadsafari.co.uk
01920 822 977

South-west

The Action Centre
www.highaction.co.uk
01934 852335

Devon Leisure
www.devon-leisure.com
01626 864315

Wales and West Midlands

Ritec Valley Quad Bikes
www.ritec-valley.co.uk
01834 843 390

Scotland

Auchterhouse Country Sports
www.treemac.co.uk
01382 320 476.

Deeside Activity Park
www.deesideactivitypark.com
013398 83536

Fyfe Off Road
www.fyfeoffroad.com
01334 472003

Westlands Activity Centre
www.westlands-activities.co.uk
01461 800 274

Northern Ireland

Adventure Tours
www.adventuretoursni.com
07971 639932

23

SKATEWING

BUZZ FOR YOUR BUCK 3/10

THRILL FACTOR ■■□□□□□□□□

Now we're not one to be behind on our adventure sports at Ride of My Life, but we're a bit baffled by this newcomer to the scene. While we're very grateful to the Germans for bringing us SCAD diving (see pages 56–58), we're not so sure about this one. See what you think. . .

A skatewing is a large, specially designed wing or sail that looks a bit like a windsurf sail and also has a boom. As the name suggests, it is designed to be used with inline skates and using the power of wind aims to give skaters some real speed . . . that is if you're strong enough to skate forward and simultaneously hold the sail directly above your head to catch the wind. In theory – and ideally you need good, constant wind – as you hold the sail above you, the wind should come from the side. When it does, you take hold of the lower boom, set the footrest on to your skate and go. In reality, we suspect you need to be built a bit like Tarzan to keep the sail horizontally above your head long enough to catch the wind.

While skatewing tends to work best on hard or tarmac surfaces, people are also experimenting using the wings with landboards on grass.

We're never ones to diss a new adventure sport so we're going to watch this one with interest. But if you've given skatewing a go and feel we're maligning the sport, then write to us and tell us. Until my postbag's full I'm inclined to stick to my skate wing pan-fried with butter and capers . . . but I'm always happy to be proved wrong.

As a new sport, the information on skatewing is limited. But for more information check out www.skatewing.com.

SKATEWING: LOOKS ODD, BUT WE HEAR IT'S FANTASTIC FUN!

24

ZORBING

BUZZ FOR YOUR BUCK 1/10
THRILL FACTOR

Have you ever wondered what it's like to be stuck in a tumble dryer? Have you ever thought, if you had the choice, that you'd prefer to be stuck in a washing machine rather than a tumble dryer? No, of course you haven't, it's only warped authors who think of things like that, and possibly those crazy Kiwis who came up with the brilliant idea of zorbing as an adventure sport.

In a nutshell – or more precisely, in a plastic ball – a zorb is a gigantic inflatable PVC ball standing about 3 metres (9 foot) in height. Inside is another smaller ball, suspended in position. As the 'zorber', you clamber into the protected inner chamber, strap yourself in and some masochistic person then pushes you down a hill. You'll see how similar it might indeed be to being stuck in a tumble dryer when you reach speeds of up to 50 km/h (31 mph) while you roll around inside and bounce down the hill. If that's not enough excitement for a lifetime, why not throw a whole heap of water into the equation and go hydro-zorbing? Rather than being strapped in, you're left sloshing around in water as you tumble down the hill, much like being stuck in a washing machine.

Zorbing is a relative newcomer to the adventure sports' world but both dry-zorbing and hydro-zorbing are becoming very popular. So all you need to do now is decide whether you'd rather be stuck in a washing machine or a tumble dryer.

GETTING INVOLVED

There are an increasing number of commercial companies offering zorbing experiences around the UK. You will need to be at the venue for about an hour, during which time you will have a safety briefing, be strapped in, have your ride and then be retrieved again.

EQUIPMENT NEEDED

For a one-off experience you'll need nothing at all, but do take a change of clothes and a towel if you are going to try the hydro-zorbing.

TEARING DOWN A HILL AT SPEEDS OF 48 KP/H (30MPH) IS EXHILARATING

WHERE TO GET INVOLVED

COMPANIES

South-west

Zorb South UK
www.zorbsouth.co.uk
01929 426 595

Wales and West Midlands

Into the Blue
www.intotheblue.co.uk
01959 578 100

Scotland

Nae Limits
(offers Sphering, which is similar but slightly different – and will still give you an incredible buzz!)
www.naelimits.co.uk
01353 727 242/01350 728 136

WATER

TOP 5 WATER SPORTS BY 'BUZZ FOR YOUR BUCK'

Rank	Sport
1	Kite surfing
2	Water skiing, wakeboarding, hydrofoiling
3	White water rafting
4	Jet Skiing
5	Coasteering

TOP 5 WATER SPORTS BY 'THRILL FACTOR'

Rank	Sport
1	Kite surfing
2	White water rafting
3	Power boating
4	Jet Skiing
5	Windsurfing

25
BODYBOARDING

WATER

BUZZ FOR YOUR BUCK 3/10
THRILL FACTOR ■■□□□□□□□□

'My whole life is centred on bodyboarding, whether coaching, writing or catching waves. From the first white water that I caught to the last time I got barrelled, it still offers the same amazing adrenaline buzz – it's really, really addictive.'

***Rob Barber**, previous European number 1, bodyboarding coach and editor of* ThreeSixty *magazine*

Surfing versus bodyboarding is something that surfers debate the world over. Which is technically more difficult? Which more fun? Which should you do? The southern Europeans seem to be voting with their boards – over half of wave riders in Spain, France and Portugal now use a bodyboard rather than a surfboard.

So, what's the difference? There are two key distinctions: the type of board used and how it is used. (Look, we never said this book was rocket science. . .).

Bodyboards are much shorter, squarer boards than surfboards. This is because you don't stand up on a bodyboard, you lie down on it or ride drop knee (one knee up, one knee down). Typically, a man's bodyboard measures 102–109 cm (40–43 inches) long, and a woman's bodyboard is about 97–104 cm (38–41 inches) in length. Unlike surfboards, bodyboards have no fins or skegs (skegs are stabilising struts or fins at the rear of the surfboard. They keep the board moving forward in a controlled manner . . . you hope!). This is because the idea of bodyboarding is not so much to ride the waves for as long as possible (as you would on a surfboard), but to execute dramatic tricks and turns before crashing back down into the brine. Waves to bodyboarders are what ramps are to skateboarders. Bodyboarders head out to sea to find their perfect waves in the same way as surfers do, but once out there you'll see them mastering a whole host of tricks and acrobatics: invert airs, reverse three-sixty airs, frog-legged airs, cutbacks, deep tubes, the El Rollo . . . and so the list of potential showmanship goes on.

So which is better, cooler and more difficult? Well, whether you're out expertly carving waves on your surfboard or executing a perfect invert air on your bodyboard, you can guarantee that on your return to the beach, the admiring stares you get will give you an adrenaline buzz nearly as impressive as the boarding itself.

GETTING INVOLVED

The beauty of bodyboarding is that it is tremendously easy to get involved. Simply buy or hire a board and get into the water. Before you go out, however, you must ensure that you're familiar with the two main currents (rip and cross shore) and any underwater conditions, such as rocks and reefs. Lifeguards will give you advice on these; alternatively, visit a surf club or surfing or bodyboarding school to learn more.

You will also need to be a good swimmer and confident that you can swim unaided when you lose your board to the vagaries of the waves. It's also important that you never surf alone and that you go to a beach where there are lifeguards on duty. Never go out after eating a meal or drinking alcohol, and always check the surf for at least 10 minutes before going in to ensure you have assessed the conditions and that you will be surfing in waters appropriate to your level of experience. The rules and code of conduct for bodyboarding and surfing can be found at www.britsurf.co.uk/html/code_of_conduct.asp.

When you're confident of the safety issues, you're ready to start bodyboarding – you don't necessarily need lessons. Simply catch a wave. It's all about trial, error, wipe-out and starting again. But should you want help and advice on catching unbroken waves, the use of swim fins and the easiest and safest way to master the sport, then bodyboarding lessons will be money and time well spent.

GETTING STARTED

Walk out until the water is at waist height. Hold the board tightly in front, with the back of the board pressing into your stomach. Turn back towards the shore and, with one eye peeled over your shoulder, dive forward on to the board as the wave hits your back, lying low on the board and adjusting your speed by pushing upwards to slow down. *Yeeee-haaaa!* – you have just caught your first wave! Now paddle back and start practising those moves – the more you practise, the more admiring the stares from the beach will be.

EQUIPMENT NEEDED

If you don't know your deck from your rail or your nose from your tail, then visit a good bodyboard school or a bodyboard-friendly surf shop. There, you'll find people who are only too happy to talk the hind legs off a surfing donkey. They'll guide you through the best boards to buy for your needs, body shape and weight. Once you're more proficient at bodyboarding, you'll also need a pair of swim fins – but don't splash out on these until you've had a couple of sessions riding the broken waves and mastered the basics, otherwise they'll prove a hindrance rather than a help.

BODYBOARDING: CATCHING YOUR FIRST WAVE IS A HUGE THRILL

WHERE TO GET INVOLVED

ADMINISTRATIVE BODIES

British Surfing Association (BSA) and British Bodyboarding Club (BBC)
www.britsurf.co.uk
01637 876474

The International Surfing Centre,
Fistral Beach, Newquay, Cornwall
TR7 1HY
E-mail: info@britsurf.co.uk

The BSA and BBC are recognised by the government as the national governing bodies for surfing and bodyboarding in the UK. They are also members of the International Surfing Association (ISA).

CLUBS AND SOCIETIES

South-east and London

Shore Surf Club
www.shoresurfclub.co.uk
01243 514774

South-west

British Longboard Union
www.britishlongboardunion.co.uk
07970 955658

Croyde Surf Club (North Devon)
www.croydesurfclub.com
01271 817862

Hotdoggers Longboarding Club (North Devon)
www.hotdoggers.co.uk
01271 328489/07787 906525

St Agnes Surf Club (north Cornwall)
www.aggiesurfclub.co.uk
01209 890060
E-mail: info@aggiesurfclub.co.uk

Watergate Bay Surf Club (north Cornwall)
www.thesurfclub.co.uk
E-mail: surfclub@121surfcoach.com

Wales and West Midlands

Welsh Coast Surf Club
www.welshcoastsurf.com
07742 332558
(Porthcawl, south-east Wales)
E-mail: admin@welshcoastsurf.com

East of England

East Anglia Surfing Association
www.eastcoastsurf.co.uk/EASA
E-mail: easa@eastcoastsurf.co.uk

East Coast Surf
www.eastcoastsurf.co.uk
01603 305511

Scotland

Granite City Surf Club
www.granitecitysurfclub.com
01224 252752
E-mail:
granitecitysurfclub@hotmail.co.uk

Surf and Watersports Club
www.surfandwatersportsclub-scotland.com
01261 815228/07867 522282
PO Box 11323, Banff links Beach, Banff, Scotland AB45 2YU

26 CANOEING AND KAYAKING

BUZZ FOR YOUR BUCK 5/10
THRILL FACTOR ■■□□□□□□□□

It's amazing to think that what started as a functional and vital form of transportation, is today one of the world's most popular water sports and an Olympic activity. But that's exactly how canoeing and kayaking has evolved.

'Is that a canoe in your pocket or are you simply pleased to see me?' 'No, it's a kayak. . .'. Many people are confused by the difference between a canoe and kayak. In simple terms, a kayak has a closed deck (apart from the hole you sit in) and is powered using a double-bladed paddle. A canoe, on the other hand, is an open boat in which you can either stand up or kneel, and is powered using a single-bladed paddle. Many people use the term 'canoeing' to describe the general sport, not to define what type of boat is used, so that's what we'll do here.

Canoeing's popularity is probably due to the huge range of activities available within the sport. It caters for every level of enjoyment or thrill, from a relaxing paddle upstream while you admire the scenery and stay dry in the boat, to negotiating white-water rapids at an exhilarating pace and returning to land soaked, but having had the time of your life.

Which type of canoeing is right for you? There are three types of water that you can canoe on, as follows:

- The placid water of lakes, canals and low gradient rivers will offer you anything from a gentle paddle up or downstream to the chance to take part in sprint or marathon racing. Canoe Polo on placid water is an increasingly popular sport, considered as fast and technical as football (but minus the premiership salaries).
- On the white water of higher gradient rivers, you can experience the exhilaration of rapids and take part in slalom and freestyle paddling, or simply enjoy the spectacular scenery during white-water touring.
- Finally, on sea and surf you can throw yourself into the popular kayak surfing (see pages 152–55).

Quite simply, canoeing is for everyone. Relax and watch the scenery go by or give yourself one of the wettest, toughest rides of your life.

PADDLE POWER!

GETTING INVOLVED

The best way to get involved in canoeing and kayaking is to join a club or society – it's more fun and much safer than starting out on your own. It will also help you explore all the different types of canoeing available. So, sign up for a weekend course, leave the city behind and have fun exploring the many great canoeing locations in the UK. We promise you won't regret it.

Once you have caught the canoeing and kayaking bug, you can sign up for one of the huge number of activity holidays available. These cater for the full range of experiences, from novice through to paddling expert. Alternatively, if you're much more competitive than this, then you might as well start training for the next Olympics.

EQUIPMENT NEEDED

Easy: a canoe or kayak, a paddle (single- or double-bladed) and a buoyancy aid. If you're taking to the rapids, you'll also need a wetsuit, trainers or wetsuit boots, and a helmet. When you're starting out, paddle sport venues will provide you with all the equipment you need. If you're already hooked and are looking to purchase your own equipment, then you can expect to pay between £250 and £850 for a kayak, depending on your requirements, and between £400 and £700 for a reasonable canoe. Paddles will cost around £40, but shop around for helmets and buoyancy aids as prices vary.

CANOEING AND KAYAKING: NOW YOU KNOW WHAT IT FEELS LIKE TO GO THROUGH A 40 DEGREE WASH

WHERE TO GET INVOLVED

ADMINISTRATIVE BODIES

East Midlands

British Canoe Union (BCU)
www.bcu.org.uk
0115 982 1100
British Canoe Union HQ, John Dudderidge House, Adbolton Lane, West Bridgford, Nottingham NG2 5AS

The BCU is the lead body for canoeing and kayaking in the UK.

Northern Ireland

Canoe Association of Northern Ireland
www.cani.org.uk
0870 2405065
Unit 2 River's Edge, 13–15 Ravenhill Road, Belfast, BT6 8DN

Scotland

Scottish Canoe Association
www.canoescotland.com
0131 3177314
Caledonia House, South Gyle, Edinburgh EH12 9DQ

Wales and West Midlands

Welsh Canoeing Association
www.welsh-canoeing.org.uk
01678 521199
Canolfan Tryweryn, Frongoch, Bala, Gwynedd, LL23 7NU

CLUBS AND SOCIETIES

South-east

Addlestone Canoe Club
www.addlestonecc.org.uk
01932 874592

Adur Canoe Club
www.adurcanoeclub.org.uk
01273 464769
c/o AOAC, Brighton Road, Shoreham by Sea, West Sussex BN43 5LT

Arun Canoe Club
www.aruncanoeclub.org.uk
E-mail: secretary@aruncanoeclub.org.uk

Banbury & District Canoe Club
www.banburycanoe.org.uk
01327 262585

Cuckmere Valley Canoe Club
www.cvcc.org.uk
01323 491289

Maidstone Canoe Club
www.maidstonecanoeclub.net
E-mail:
memsec@maidstonecanoeclub.net

Tonbridge Canoe Club
www.btinternet.com/~colin.duff/medway-accessdetails.htm
01732 361759
The Membership Secretary, 9 Handel Walk, Tonbridge, Kent TN10 4DG

Wokingham Canoe Club
www.wokinghamcanoeclub.co.uk
E-mail:
info@wokinghamcanoeclub.co.uk

WHERE TO GET INVOLVED

South-west

Bideford Canoe Club
www.bidefordcanoeclub.co.uk
01237 475430

Exeter Canoe Club
www.exetercanoeclub.org.uk
01392 433811

Poole Harbour Canoe Club
www.phcc.org.uk
E-mail: info@phcc.org.uk

Totnes Canoe Club
www.totnescanoeclub.org.uk
01803 520485

Wales and West Midlands

Birmingham Canoe Club
www.birminghamcanoeclub.co.uk
01922 410424
E-mail:
info@birminghamcanoeclub.co.uk

Hereford Kayak Club
www.herefordkayakclub.org.uk
01432 275528

Solihull Canoe Club
www.solihullcanoeclub.co.uk
0121 7063856
The Clubhouse, Grand Union Canal
Towpath, Off Hampton Lane,
Catherine-de-Barnes, Solihull

Snowdonia Canoe Club
www.snowdoniacanoeclub.co.uk
07790 221384

Rugby Canoe Club
www.rugbycanoeclub.org.uk

Welshpool Canoe Club
www.welshpoolcanoeclub.org.uk
01938 810532

East Midlands

Lincoln Canoe Club
www.lincolncanoeclub.co.uk

Matlock Canoe Club
www.matlockcanoeclub.co.uk
01773 780514

Northampton Canoe and Kayak Club
www.nckc.org.uk
01604 753357

Rutland Canoe Club
www.rutlandcanoeclub.org.uk
01476 860609

East of England

Herts Canoe Club
www.hertscanoeclub.org.uk

North of England

Bradford and Bingley Canoe Club
www.bradbingcc.org.uk
01756 791648

Carlisle Canoe Club
www.carlislecanoeclub.org.uk
07746 025187
E-mail: Info@CarlisleCanoeClub.org.uk

Clitheroe Canoe Club
www.clitheroecanoeclub.org.uk
01254 822440

Durham Kayak Club
www.durhamkayakclub.org.uk
E-mail:
durhamkayakclub@hotmail.co.uk

WHERE TO GET INVOLVED

Leeds Canoe Club
www.leedscanoeclub.co.uk
01302 390718

West Cumbria Canoe Club
www.westcumbriacanoeclub.org.uk
01900 826691

Scotland

Angus Canoe Club
www.anguscanoeclub.org.uk
01674 840437

Edinburgh Kayak Club
www.edinburghkayak.com
0131 453 4479
E-mail: info@edinburghkayak.com

Forth Canoe Club
www.forthcc.com
07867 788919

Lochwinnoch & Paisley Kayak Club
www.lpkc.co.uk
01505 842442

Nithsdale Canoe Club
www.nithsdalecanoeclub.org.uk
01387 263505

Pentland Canoe Club
www.pentlandcanoeclub.org.uk
01847 831508

Northern Ireland

Foyle Paddlers Canoe Club
www.foylepaddlers.org.uk
028 71348202
E-mail:
information@foylepaddlers.org.uk

27 CANYONING

BUZZ FOR YOUR BUCK 7/10
THRILL FACTOR

If jumping off cliffs 7-metres (23-feet) high, sliding down natural river slides and abseiling down waterfalls 15–20 metres (49–66 feet) high is your idea of having fun, then the sport of canyoning is right up your ravine.

Canyoning is the salt-free version of coasteering (which as the name suggests takes place along the UK coastline; see also pages 138–41). Walk, scramble, abseil and swim down rivers or streams within a canyon or ravine and you're guaranteed a fantastic thrill amidst spectacular scenery. The aim of the sport is to traverse the landscape in the best and safest way possible. To do canyoning really well and safely, you'll need to develop navigation, rope-work and climbing skills. You'll get wet, possibly even a bit cold, but none of this should put you off as you jump into your next plunge pool or negotiate a narrow, fast-flowing gorge.

The beauty of this sport is that most people can do it. You need just a reasonable level of fitness, a head for heights and an appreciation for stunning scenery. Being able to swim will definitely help, but this isn't a prerequisite as flotation devices are normally provided.

GETTING INVOLVED

Head to Scotland or Wales for some of the best canyoning sites in the UK. Several commercial companies offer one- or half-day canyoning trips to whet (literally) your appetite. Safety briefings and equipment will be provided, so all you need to bring is a spirit of adventure and fun.

Canyoning is not a sport to do on your own or without someone who has good knowledge of local geography and conditions. There are considerable risks involved so you must *always* canyon with a group of people including a qualified instructor. Working as part of a group will make your experience safer and, therefore, more enjoyable. In addition, different members of the group bring different skills to the adventure, making your canyoning day more varied and exciting.

CANYONING: TAKE THE PLUNGE!

EQUIPMENT NEEDED

When canyoning with an organised group, you will be provided with a wetsuit, waterproof top, helmet, buoyancy aid and first aid kit. These are all essential for any canyoning trip. You will need to take along spare, dry footwear, swimwear, some warm clothes to put on over the wetsuit and a change of clothes.

CAN YOU CANYON? YES, YOU CAN!

WHERE TO GET INVOLVED

ADMINISTRATIVE BODIES

There are hard and fast rules and regulations for activities such as rock climbing, mountain leading and canoeing, but there's no governing body for canyoning. It comes under the umbrella of the British Mountaineering Council (BMC), and is recognised as an activity that qualified mountain guides are capable of instructing people in.

British Mountaineering Council (BMC)
www.thebmc.co.uk
0870 0104878
177–179 Burton Road, Manchester, M20 2BB

CLUBS, SOCIETIES AND COMPANIES

Wales and West Midlands
Adventure Activities
www.outdooradventureactivities.com
01341 241275

Scotland

Activ8s
www.activ8s.com
01887 829292
The Coachyard, Aberfeldy, Perthshire, PH15 2AS

Arran Adventure Company
www.arranadventure.com
01770 302244

Freespirits
www.freespirits-online.co.uk
0845 6444755
The Riverside Inn, Grandtully By Pitlochry, Perthshire, PH15 0PL

Nae Limits
www.naelimits.co.uk
01350 727242
14, The Cross, Dunkeld, PH8 0AJ

Wild Spirits
www.wildspirits.co.uk
0870 760 7582
Unit 34, Sir James Clark Building, Abby Mill Industrial Estate, Paisley PA1 1TJ

Northern Ireland

Mourne Activity Breaks
028 41769965
28 Bridge Street, Kilkeel, Co. Down
E-mail:
info@mourneactivitybreaks.co.uk

28

COASTEERING

BUZZ FOR YOUR BUCK 7/10
THRILL FACTOR ■■■■■□□□□□

Coasteering is the official sporting name for an activity that's a cross between all the things you weren't supposed to do on childhood seaside holidays and a daring day out for the Famous Five. A close, salty relation to canyoning (see pages 134–7), coasteering will have you scrambling over and around the rocks or cliff faces of a coastline, then jumping off cliffs into the foaming waters below.

Using a combination of trekking, climbing, scrambling, cliff jumping and swimming, the aim of a coasteering session is to traverse along the bottom of cliffs using rocks and water, and work out the best route with your team and instructor. When the going's too steep, you'll need to jump into the waters below and swim to the next easy climbing spot.

Summer is the most popular time of year for this sport, although if you live in the UK you'll know not to expect Mediterranean temperatures. People who have been bitten by the coasteering bug and have more experience under their helmet will often choose to do the sport later into the autumn, when there's more chance of swell, which brings an added adrenaline buzz.

If you like swimming, love the sea and want an adrenaline-filled 'Famous Five' adventure, then pack up your ginger beer and head to your nearest coasteering centre. As Julian, Dick, Anne and George would say, this really is 'a jolly good sport'.

GETTING INVOLVED

Britain's coastline offers countless exciting opportunities for coasteering. But first, you will need to find a company that offers the correct – and absolutely essential – equipment, training and supervision. As with canyoning, this is very much a group sport; you'll be guided in appropriate-sized groups according to the levels of ability within the group. Staff will keep a close eye on you and encourage you to push yourself bit by bit, so that you step out of your comfort zone.

You'll need to start slowly. During beginner level sessions, you'll be shown the correct and safest way to jump and then will need to practise several times by jumping into protected rock pools. As you become more confident and participate in intermediate and advanced sessions, you will jump higher – up to 10 metres (33 feet), and even higher in some places. The good thing

COASTEERING: AN ADRENALIN COCKTAIL

about coasteering is that there is no pressure for those who might be nervous about doing the higher jumps. With the encouragement of staff and fellow group members, people develop confidence gradually, and probably find themselves jumping from heights they initially never thought they would – not to mention feeling an adrenaline rush they never thought they'd feel.

Although anyone can give this sport a try, a day's coasteering will be physically demanding, so a certain level of stamina and fitness is required. Scrambling over rocks, climbing cliffs and swimming against swells take their toll. But, by the end of the day, you are guaranteed a large grin and some seaweed on your face. A half day will cost from £40, and if you feel up to a full day then expect to pay upwards of £70.

EQUIPMENT NEEDED

The equipment you need will depend on the coastline you're tackling. Always contact the company you are going with in advance. Most will provide all the safety equipment you will need and, at the time of booking, should give you a list of any additional kit that you will need to take. The wetsuit and buoyancy aid will keep you afloat so the sport is accessible to non-swimmers and those nervous about the water. If you don't need a wetsuit for the area you're in, you'll want to take some old, comfortable clothes that you don't mind getting wet and dirty. It's also recommended that you wear closed trainers that you're happy to get wet. Always ring the company you are going with in advance, to check whether you need additional kit.

WHERE TO GET INVOLVED

ADMINISTRATIVE BODIES

There is no national governing body for coasteering.

COMPANIES

South-west

The Adventure Centre
www.adventure-centre.org
01637 872444
Lusty Glaze Beach, Lusty Glaze Road, Newquay, Cornwall TR7 3AE

WHERE TO GET INVOLVED

Essential Adventure
www.essential-adventure.co.uk
01395 271156
(Devon)
E-mail: info@essential-adventure.co.uk

Penhale Adventure Centre
www.penhaleadventure.com
0800 781 6861
Building 75, Penhale Training Camp, Holywell Bay, Newquay, Cornwall TR8 5PF

Wales and West Midlands

Celtic Watersports
www.surf-kayaking.co.uk
0845 0563902

The National Watersports Centre
www.plasmenai.co.uk
01248 673943
E-mail: info@plasmenai.co.uk

Pembrokeshire Activity Centre
www.pembrokeshire-activity-centre.co.uk
01646 622013
E-mail: pac@princes-trust.org.uk

Preseli Venture
www.preseliventure.com
01348 837709
Preseli Venture, Parcynole Fach, Mathry, Haverfordwest, Pembrokeshire SA62 5HN
E-mail: info@preseliventure.com

Proactive Adventure
www.proactive-adventure.com
01588 630123
The Old Forge Annex, Snead, Churchstoke, Powys SY15 6EB

Shaggy Sheep Wales
www.shaggysheepwales.co.uk
07919 244549
Cilwen House, Carmarthen SA33 5RH

TYF Adventure
www.tyf.com
01437 721611
1 High Street, St Davids, Pembrokeshire, SA62 6SA

Scotland

Hebridean Pursuits Ltd
www.hebrideanpursuits.com
01631 710317
Grosvenor Crescent, Connel, Oban, Argyll PA37 1PQ

Uist Outdoor Centre
www.uistoutdoorcentre.co.uk
01876 500480
Cearn Dusgaidh, Lochmaddy, Isle of North Uist HS6 5AE

Northern Ireland

Bluelough
www.mountainandwater.com
028 4377 0714
The Grange Yard, Castlewellan Forest Park, Castlewellan, Co. Down, BT31 9BU

Mourne Activity Breaks
028 41769965
28 Bridge Street, Kilkeel, Co. Down
E-mail:
info@mourneactivitybreaks.co.uk

29

DINGHY SAILING

BUZZ FOR YOUR BUCK 5/10
THRILL FACTOR

To the uninitiated, dinghy sailing might conjure up rather tame thoughts of *Swallows and Amazons* or 'We are the champions' pool-based inflatables. Adventurous – yeah, right! Wrong. Instead, think Ben Ainslie racing his way to Olympic victory. What could be more adventurous than pitting your wits against the waves, currents and wind? You must harness and master the elements as they try to take control of your boat, and balance by changing position of the crew. Skipping across the waves at speeds that have to be experienced to be understood will leave your heart pounding.

The layman's perspective of dinghy sailing might be that it's always been a 'gentleman's' sport. And you may well be right, when you consider that back in the nineteenth century, when the Royal Yachting Association (RYA) was founded, membership was a right reserved for the 'well-to-do'. To a certain extent this is still true, but dinghy sailing is losing its image of exclusivity. In fact, the number of participants is mounting; junior members sometimes outnumber adult members in UK clubs.

There's years of fun and adrenaline-fuelled adventure to be had in dinghy sailing, at whatever level you wish to take part. There are clubs and competitions for every category of boat, so while you're out on the water practicing manoeuvres and ensuring your 'course is made good', you could be well on your way to winning your dream race.

GETTING INVOLVED

Despair ye not, as dinghy sailing really is accessible to all. A small, second-hand dinghy costs a few hundred pounds; a new boat will set you back in the region of £1000. If you want to try before you buy, simply hire one at the many centres throughout the UK. Beginner RYA courses are plentiful up and down the country, both on the coast and at inland lakes and rivers. Depending on the time you have available and how quickly you want to learn, you can take half-day courses, day courses, weekend courses, week-long courses and even sailing holiday courses. Expect to pay around £100 for a day. The RYA Level 1 course, which will teach you the basics for dinghy sailing, will cost between £150 and £200.

GREAT BRITAIN'S CHRIS DRAPER AND SIMON HISCOCKS ON THEIR WAY TO WINNING BRONZE

Sizes and types of boat vary massively, but generally fall into the following broad types:

- First, there's the skiff, which is the fastest dinghy on the water.
- Next, are high-performance dinghies. These are designed for racing around an Olympic course.
- Third, cruising dinghies are designed for leisure and family sailing.
- Finally, there are the many classes of catamaran, sports boat and racing dinghies.

TAKING IT FURTHER

There are sailing clubs a-plenty in the UK and no shortage of events and races to try your hand at. Most races and regattas are categorised based on the class of dinghy, and there may be further divisions within that such as Masters, Ladies and Juniors.

Once you're hooked and want to buy a dingy, consider first whether you want to race. If the answer is yes, then check out your local sailing clubs to see what type of dinghy is popular, as it is more fun racing against large numbers and you'll probably learn more. Also, do you want to sail alone? Single crew dinghies allow you to sail when you want, but those requiring two crew allow you to share the expense and experience. And, finally, does your dinghy need to be car portable or will it be based at one location?

EQUIPMENT NEEDED

Obviously the hardware is pretty important when it comes to sailing, as is a wetsuit, drysuit or waterproof clothing (depending on the dinghy you're sailing) and a life jacket. The kit that is needed will vary from sunscreen to extra jumpers depending on the type of sailing, the time of year and location. As a beginner, sailing clubs and centres will hire you all the kit you need. Making a success of dinghy sailing also depends on your grey matter (tactics based on your understanding of the weather conditions), so prepare well before you go out on the water.

WHERE TO GET INVOLVED

ADMINISTRATIVE BODIES

Royal Yachting Association (RYA)
www.rya.org.uk
023 8060 4100
RYA House, Ensign Way, Hamble, Southampton, Hampshire, SO31 4YA

The RYA is recognised as the national governing body for sailing in the UK.

CLUBS AND SOCIETIES

South-east and London

Bosham Sailing Club
www.boshamsailingclub.co.uk
01243 572341

Dover Water Sports Centre
www.doverwatersports.com
01304 212880

Hythe (Southampton) Sailing club
www.hythesailingclub.org.uk
02380 893604

Portsmouth Outdoor Centre
www.portsmouthoutdoor.co.uk
023 9266 3873

Queen Mary Sailing Club
www.queenmary.org.uk
01784 248881

Rockley Watersports
www.rockleywatersports.com
0870 7770541

South-west

Fowey Maritime Centre
www.foweymaritimecentre.com
01726 833924

Penhale Adventure Centre
www.penhaleadventure.com
0800 781 6861

Weymouth and Portland National Sailing Academy
www.wpnsa.org.uk
01305 866000

Wales and West Midlands

Bala Sailing Club
www.balasc.org.uk
01678 520118

Croft Farm Waterpark
www.croftfarmleisure.co.uk
01684 772321

The National Watersports Centre
www.plasmenai.co.uk
01248 673943

Pembrokeshire Activity Centre
www.pembrokeshire-activity-centre.co.uk
01646 622013

East Midlands

Carsington Sailing Club
www.carsingtonsc.co.uk
01629 540609

Nottinghamshire County Sailing Club
www.ncsc.org.uk
01636 830065

WHERE TO GET INVOLVED

Rutland Watersports
www.anglianwaterleisure.co.uk
01780 460154

Rutland Sailing School
www.rutlandsailingschool.co.uk
01780 721999

East of England

Orford Sailing Club
www.orfordsail.org.uk
01394 450997

Northern England

Coquet Shorebase Trust
www.coquetshorebase.org.uk
01665 710367

North Lincolnshire and Humberside Sailing Club
www.nlsail.co.uk
01652 632514

Windermere Outdoor Adventure
www.southlakelandleisure.org.uk/windermere
015394 47183

Scotland

Royal Findhorn Yacht Club
www.royalfindhornyachtclub.com
01309 691728

Scottish National Sports Centre Cumbrae
www.nationalcentrecumbrae.org.uk
01475 530757

Northern Ireland

Holywood Yacht Club
www.hyc.org.uk
028 9042 3345

30

JET SKIING

BUZZ FOR YOUR BUCK 8/10
THRILL FACTOR

'Most people have dreams, I'm fortunate enough to be living mine. Becoming the Jet Ski World Champion at fourteen years old, along with winning many other titles, was truly amazing.'

***Lee Stone**, Jet Ski World Champion 2005*

Lying on a beach while jet skiers rip around the sea is about as peaceful as relaxing on the grid at Brands Hatch. However, in spite of their ear-shattering similarity to a swarm of hornets screeching through super-woofer speakers (making them as popular as a rash), jet skis are very much here to stay. In fact, it's estimated that by the end of the 1990s, there were over 18,000 jet skis in the UK. Rather like motocross on water, jet skiing has become a hugely popular and much-practised motor sport in its own right.

You'll find jet skiers in the UK practising on rivers, inland lakes and coastal sites. And, to clear up any confusion, jet skiers are the ones who stand on their skis; jet bikers take it easy and sit down. So, for jet skiing, you'll need to master the skill of weight distribution as you learn how to handle your personal water craft (PWC), or 'ski.'

Although you might think of jet skiing as a half-hour holiday activity, it can be far from this. Once you feel reasonably confident on a PWC, then it's time to push yourself to the next step and enjoy the competitive exhilaration of racing. Racing is increasingly popular and highly competitive; the British, Irish and European Championships are precursors to the World Finals. But you don't need to have years of experience or be riding the best and most expensive jet ski on the market to take part. You'll find that there are different competition classes that allow most people on most skis to race. Then there's also the adrenaline-fuelled world of freestyle – a great, heart-stopping spectator sport. Jet-ski freestyle sees participants performing an incredible routine of different tricks such as Big Air, Hand Stands, Back Flips, Corkscrews

JET SKIERS DO IT STANDING UP

and the politically incorrectly-named Wife Soakers! Competitors are judged on the quality and skill displayed in their routines. Furthermore, jet skiing is a popular spectator sport across the UK.

If you like the idea of a sport that mixes water skiing with speedboat driving and throws in the potential speed thrills of motorcycle racing, then jet skiing is probably for you.

GETTING INVOLVED

For an introductory experience, visit a commercial water sports centre in the UK for a lesson on a hired ski. If this whets your appetite and you want to advance your skills, sign up for the RYA's Personal Watercraft Course. This normally takes a day to complete and will teach you safe, confident and responsible use of personal watercraft. You'll also learn about high- and low-speed riding skills, essential safety information, collision avoidance and orientation at sea. Expect to pay upwards of £100 for the day's course. On successful completion of the Personal Watercraft Course, you'll be awarded a certificate which is required for launching in most UK harbours and is also needed if you want to use your PWC abroad. (If you buy a new PWC, you will be given a voucher towards the cost of this course.)

LEE STONE PERFORMS HAIR-RAISING STUNTS ON HIS JET SKI

For a new, all-singing, all-speeding jet ski, prices start at around £5000 for a basic model and quickly rise into the tens of thousands. However, there is a good second-hand market in the UK which is worth checking out.

EQUIPMENT NEEDED

What's needed? A sense of adventure and a love of life in the fast lane. So, get on board, get out on the water and jet ski for your life! And, as the fastest mouse in Mexico, Speedy Gonzales, would say, '*Arriba! Arriba!*'

WHERE TO GET INVOLVED

ADMINISTRATIVE BODIES

Royal Yachting Association (RYA)
www.rya.org.uk
0845 345 0400
RYA House, Ensign Way, Hamble, Southampton, Hampshire SO31 4YA

The RYA is the UK's national association for all forms of recreational and competitive boating, including personal watercraft.

CLUBS AND SCHOOLS

The following clubs offer the RYA Personal Watercraft Course, designed for first-time and experienced riders alike. Most courses take one day and teach safe, confident and responsible use of personal watercraft. They cover high- and low-speed riding skills, essential safety information, collision avoidance and orientation at sea.

South-east

Bembridge Sailing Club
www.bembridgesailingclub.org
01983 872237
Embankment Road, Bembridge, Isle of Wight PO35 5NR

Herne Bay SCC Watersports Centre
www.watercrafttraining.co.uk
07845 959766
Hampton Pier, Herne Bay, Kent CT6 8EP

South-west

PWC Training UK
www.pwctraining.com
01736 757555/07870 728281
Unit 11, Octel Building, North Quay, Hayle Harbour, Cornwall TR7 24B

Torbay and Dartmouth Powerboat School
www.powerboat-instruction.co.uk
01803 855508
Ostend House, 1 King Street, Brixham, Devon , TQ5 9TF

WHERE TO GET INVOLVED

Wales and West Midlands

Colwyn Jet Ski Club
www.colwynjetskiclub.co.uk
07786 036620

Kingsbury Jet Bike Centre
www.jet-bike.com
01827 874815 or 07968 748734
Hemlingford Lake, Kingsbury Water Park, Bodymoor Heath Lane, Sutton Coldfield, B76 0DY

Swansea Watersports
www.swanseawatersports.com
07989 839878
The Pilot House, Pilot Wharf, Swansea Marina, Swansea SA1 1UN

East of England

Southend Marine Activities Centre
www.southendmarineactivitiescentre.co.uk
01702 612770
Eastern Esplanade, Southend-on-Sea, Essex SS1 2YH

Tallington Lakes
www.tallington.com
01778 347000
E-mail: info@tallington.com

North of England

Safe Water Training Sea School
www.safewater.co.uk
0151 630 0466
68 Victoria Parade, New Brighton, Wirral CH45 2PH

Scotland

Jet Ski Ecosse
www.jetskiecosse.co.uk
01294 279978
(Irvine, near Kilmarnock)

Seaforce
www.seaforce.co.uk
0141 221 1070
Glasgow Harbour, 100 Stobcross Road, Glasgow G3 8QQ

Sea Skills
www.seaskills.co.uk
01620 895135 (after 6pm)
45 High Street, North Berwick, East Lothian E39 4HH

31 KAYAK SURFING

BUZZ FOR YOUR BUCK 6/10
THRILL FACTOR

'Surf kayaking is, in my eyes, the most dynamic and exhilarating discipline of kayaking, combining the sheer excitement of kayaking with the cool lifestyle of surfing. Give it a go; every time you get out on the water, you'll be grinning from ear to ear.'

***Nathan Eades**, previous British Kayak Surfing Champion and former World number 2*

As the name suggests, kayak surfing involves surfing in kayaks (I know, I know . . . you didn't pay good money for this book so that the authors could state the blindingly obvious. . .). But these aren't just any old kayaks – they're specially designed to allow you to perform the same skilled manoeuvres as a surfer.

In spite of the fact that kayak surfing has been undertaken to a high level in the UK for over fifteen years, with teams competing exceptionally well at world level and several Brits holding World Championship titles, kayak surfing has had a far lower profile than traditional surfing. Fortunately, this lack of publicity is set to change – kayak surfing is currently only second to the more sedate sea kayaking as the paddle sport with the fastest rate of uptake.

So, if you love the sea and are looking for a sport that offers you the exhilaration of tackling waves with the challenge of technical, high performance moves, why not join the growing band of kayak surfers? After a few lessons, you'll be leaping into your kayak, riding the waves and performing bottom turns, top turns, cut backs, round-house cut backs, tail slashes, lip turns and even 'the Bouncer'. Once you've mastered these skills, all that will remain is for you to brace yourself to ignore the gags about kayak surfing being for surfers who can't stand up.

GETTING INVOLVED

You can expect to pick up the basics of kayak surfing in a few days, but to really master the sport will take a lifetime. That said, you'll find that even as a shaky beginner you'll have great fun, and experience a real buzz from the challenges the waves present and the tricks you try to master. Try an introductory weekend to the sport to see if it's for you, but book early – the

BRITISH CHAMPION NATHAN EADES TACKLES THE WAVES IN HIS KAKAK (PHOTOGRAPHER: DUNCAN EADES)

centres and clubs that run them are usually highly oversubscribed. Expect to pay in the region of £150–£200, and any additional costs for accommodation if it is not included, for a weekend introductory course.

Once hooked, you'll find that you can enter numerous competitions across the UK, with opportunities at a top level to be selected for National Teams.

EQUIPMENT NEEDED

The equipment list for kayaking is brief and most clubs and schools will provide it for you. The most important piece of kit is the specially designed kayak, although as a beginner you'll find a standard kayak or a playboat (anything less than 2.5 metres/8 feet in length) are better as they are less twitchy and easier to roll. To accompany the kayak, you'll need paddles, spray deck (the important stretchy thing you have to squeeze yourself into and then fix around the hole where you sit so the water doesn't get in the craft and sink it), buoyancy aid, helmet and wet suit. If you're hooked to the point of wanting to purchase your own equipment, prices start at around £250 for a specially designed kayak plus all the gear.

WHERE TO GET INVOLVED

ADMINISTRATIVE BODIES

British Canoe Union (BCU)
www.bcu.org.uk
0115 982 1100
British Canoe Union HQ, John Dudderidge House, Adbolton Lane, West Bridgford, Nottingham NG2 5AS

The BCU is the lead body for canoeing and kayaking in the UK.

CLUBS AND SOCIETIES

South-east

Adur Canoe Club
www.adurcanoeclub.org.uk
01273 464769
c/o AOAC, Brighton Road, Shoreham by Sea, West Sussex BN43 5LT

Arun Canoe Club
www.aruncanoeclub.org.uk
01903 525181
E-mail:
secretary@aruncanoeclub.org.uk

Cuckmere Valley Canoe Club
www.cvcc.org.uk
01323 491289

WHERE TO GET INVOLVED

South-west

Bideford Canoe Club
www.bidefordcanoeclub.co.uk
01237 475430

Exeter Canoe Club
www.exetercanoeclub.org.uk
01392 433811

Poole Harbour Canoe Club
www.phcc.org.uk
E-mail: info@phcc.org.uk

Wales

Celtic Watersports
www.surf-kayaking.co.uk
0845 0563902

Snowdonia Canoe Club
www.snowdoniacanoeclub.co.uk
07790 221384

Welshpool Canoe Club
www.welshpoolcanoeclub.org.uk
01938 810532

East Midlands

Rutland Canoe Club
www.rutlandcanoeclub.org.uk
01476 860609

North of England

Bradford and Bingley Canoe Club
www.bradbingcc.org.uk
01756 791648

Carlisle Canoe Club
www.carlislecanoeclub.org.uk
07746 025187
E-mail: Info@CarlisleCanoeClub.org.uk

Durham Kayak Club
www.durhamkayakclub.org.uk
E-mail:
durhamkayakclub@hotmail.co.uk

Leeds Canoe Club
www.leedscanoeclub.co.uk
01302 390718

Scotland

Edinburgh Kayak Club
www.edinburghkayak.com
0131 453 4479
E-mail: info@edinburghkayak.com

Forth Canoe Club
www.forthcc.com
07867 788919

Lochwinnoch & Paisley Kayak Club
www.lpkc.co.uk
01505 842442

Nithsdale Canoe Club
www.nithsdalecanoeclub.org.uk
01387 263505

Pentland Canoe Club
www.pentlandcanoeclub.org.uk
01847 831508

Northern Ireland

Canoe Association of Northern Ireland
www.cani.org.uk
0870 240 5065

Foyle Paddlers Canoe Club
www.foylepaddlers.org.uk
028 71348202
E-mail:
information@foylepaddlers.org.uK

32

KITE SURFING

BUZZ FOR YOUR BUCK 9/10
THRILL FACTOR

'I first started kitesurfing when I was eleven years old. I have been hooked ever since but have never come close to that same rush and enjoyment in any other sport. The lifestyle and fun that accompanies this sport is unreal, so get out there and go for it. For sure you will be hooked straight away.'

Aaron Hadlow, *3 times World Champion*

Kite surfing, also known as kite boarding, may be the ultimate sport for those who want to experience the speed of a water sport and the power of an air sport. Indeed, kite surfing harnesses the two, resulting in a cross between paragliding and wakeboarding or surfing. The overall effect is a challenging sport of speed, height, skill, stunts and sheer excitement. Kite surfing is one of the fastest growing, best, greatest, most exhilarating, electrifying, top sports in the UK – plus 50 other superlatives you can think of to describe it. (Do you get the impression we're either totally sold on this one or own shares in a kite surfing company?)

Kite surfers can reach speeds of 50 km/h (30 mph) on flat water with very little wind. A de-powerable kite (inflatable kite) is flown at approximately 45 degrees to the board, to generate the power needed to speed across the water, jump waves and even fly through the air (though the latter is dangerous and should only be attempted by seasoned kite surfers). As the kite surfer, you'll be attached to the board by footstraps and attached to the kite by a strong harness on four 30-metre (98-feet) lines; you'll use a bar like a water ski bar to steer, de-power and disable the kite.

Kite surfing is definitely a sport where you need the ability to multi-task, as you're the only connection between the board and the kite, although the harness will take much of the power. Piloting them both is an exhilarating challenge, the conquering of which guarantees an unforgettable high. When the kite's flying high and the board's skimming across the water, you'll be leaping waves, jumping and turning high in mid-air. At such times you may well have reached the adventure sports nirvana; you'll have certainly reached god/goddess-like status with the onlookers on the beach.

KITE SURFING: THERE SHE BLOWS!

Kite surfing is a relative newcomer to the adventure sports scene, invented by the French and popularised by the Hawaiians in the late 1990s. But the newcomer has wasted no time making its presence felt:

in 1998 there were estimated to be a mere 30 kite surfers worldwide, but by 2006 that figure had grown to somewhere between 150,000 and 200,000. And it continues to grow. The UK has also produced its own kite surfing heroes: previous three-time World Champion Mark Shinn has kite surfed from Spain to Morocco, and Aaron Hadlow is the current three-time World Champion (2004, 2005 and 2006).

GETTING INVOLVED

First, to kite surf you'll need good technique and stamina, and to be a good swimmer. Second, kite surfing is not a sport you can do without initial training and guidance. A background in water sports and kite flying will help. Apart from all the kit that will need to be demonstrated to you, it's also a potentially dangerous sport so you must invest in lessons from a qualified instructor; we strongly recommend training through the British Kite Surfing Association (BKSA) at a BKSA-approved school. A short course will be the safest but also the quickest way to get you out on the water. Most novices will be up and kite surfing after a 2- or 3-day course; expect to pay around £200 plus for this. Once you've completed your initial training, it's a good idea to join a local club where fellow members with more kite surfing experience will be able to offer you advice and support.

EQUIPMENT NEEDED

Centres and schools offering courses for beginners will provide all the equipment you need to learn to kite surf. Once you're hooked and want to invest in some of your own kit, then go to a good kite surfing shop. Many shops offer beginners' packages, to include a board and kite complete with bar and lines; some shops also offer wetsuits and harnesses as part of the package. These specialist shops will also be able to give you in-depth advice on the size of kite you need, this being dependent on your weight. Expect to pay around £1500 for a board and kite and, if you choose to buy second-hand, about £600 upwards.

In addition to this, you might want to buy wetsuit boots to protect your feet and we strongly recommend you wear a helmet at all times while kite surfing. A buoyancy aid will not only help you stay afloat, it will provide additional warmth and help reduce the impact of the water if you wipe out.

WHERE TO GET INVOLVED

ADMINISTRATIVE BODIES

British Kite Surfing Association (BKSA)
www.kitesurfing.org
01305 813555
BKSA, PO Box 7871, East Leake, Leicestershire LE12 6WL
E-mail: info@kitesurfing.org

The BKSA is the governing body for kite surfing in the UK. A comprehensive up-to-date list of schools and shops is available on the BKSA website.

CLUBS, SOCIETIES AND COMPANIES

South-east and London

Essex Kite Surf School
www.essexkitesurfschool.co.uk
07751 705558

Hayling Kitesurfing Association
www.hka.org.uk
02392 460555

Hayling Island Kite Surf School
www.hikitesurfschool.co.uk
02392 422570

Transition Kiteboarding
www.transitionkiteboarding.com
02083 782138

X-Isle Kite Surfing School
www.x-is.co.uk
01983 873111

X-Train
www.x-train.co.uk
01243 513077

Zero Gravity Kite School
www.zerogravityextreme.co.uk
02392 460555

South-west

Edge Watersports Kite School
www.edgewatersports.com
01395 222551

Extreme Academy
www.extremeacademy.co.uk
01637 860840

FCWatersports Academy
www.fcwatersports.co.uk
01202 708283

Mobius Kitesurfing School
www.mobiusonline.co.uk
01637 831383

Paracademy
www.paracademy.co.uk
1305 824797

Penhale Adventure Centre
www.penhaleadventure.com
0800 781 6861
Torquay Kite School
www.kitesurfing-torquaywindsurfing.co.uk
01803 212411.

Wales and West Midlands

Big Blue Kite Surfing School
www.bigbluesurfing.com
07816 169359

WATER

WHERE TO GET INVOLVED

FKS Kitesurf School
www.fks.me.uk
01407 810598

East of England

The Hub
www.kitesurfhub.org
07957 628715

Northern England

Surfstore
www.surfstore.co.uk
01740 631199

Scotland

Kite Sports Scotland Ltd
www.kss.uk.com
07875 773346

YOUR BODY IS THE ONLY CONNECTION BETWEEN THE KITE AND THE BOARD . . . ARE YOU UP TO IT?

33

POWER BOATING

WATER

BUZZ FOR YOUR BUCK 3/10

THRILL FACTOR

Power boating is about knowing your inshore from your offshore, your Thundercats from your hydroplanes, and about dreaming of *Miami Vice* not *Swallows and Amazons*. But it's not just a simple case of turning up, leaping on board and pushing the throttle north; first, you need to decide which sort of power boat you want to board and what you want to do with it.

Lots of peole just want to experience the one-off thrill of screaming over the waves at top speeds; to do this, a commercial company will take you out on the water for a couple of hours. There are plenty of companies all over the UK with a variety of power boats, and you will certainly have a fantastic experience. But, for those of you who really want to feel your adrenaline pumping, why not take it further and get into the serious thrills of the racing circuit?

This is all about fast and furious racing on closed, protected inland lakes and rivers. Think it's too expensive? Think again. For as little as £2500 you could be driving your very own Thundercat boat at speeds of around

80 km/h (50 mph) and setting your sights on competing in the World Championships.

Thundercats and Zapcats

Thundercats are funky, fast, inflatable boats, and there is a growing global community of racers. While on the water, the racing is taken very seriously indeed, but off the water the focus is on having fun with friends and family. Originally invented in South Africa about 20 years ago, Thundercat racing, otherwise known as 'Inflatable boat racing', is hugely popular in the Southern hemisphere; during the last 7 years its has finally made it over to our cooler shores in the UK. Inflatable racing is a high-adrenaline team sport in which the pilot drives/navigates, while the co-pilot uses their weight and agility around the boat to stabilise it and gain maximum speed. There are three disciplines within the championship; circuit flat water, offshore surf and endurance long hauls.

Zapcat racing is a one-design series based on Inflatable P750 boat racing, but in this class all the boats are exactly the same design and specification. With the boats deflating to a quarter of their original length, you can even get them into the back of most estate cars for easy transportation.

THUNDERCATS ARE GO!

Both Thundercats and Zapcats are a relatively cheap powerboat (relative, that is, to the thrill and speed) if you want to enter the racing circuit. But don't think it's all plain sailing once you've bought your boat: you'll need to be fit and have good upper body strength to race and get the best out of these boats.

Hydroplanes and sports boats

However, if 80 km/h (50 mph) is closer to the speed of your stumble home from the pub on a Friday night, then how about taking to the water in a hydroplane? If you have a spare £8000 to £20,000, you can buy a boat that will allow you to drive at around 115–160 km/h (70–100 mph) and compete in races both around the UK and across the world. Still too sedentary? Then you could splash out on an NS 2000/F2 for about £30,000 and join the sports boat class. You'll be able to let rip at 195 km/h (120 mph) as you sit restrained inside a safety cell in the boat (then try telling us that your heart rate hasn't gone through the roof. . .).

Offshore racing

Perhaps the best known type of powerboat racing is offshore racing. This is nearly as exciting for the spectators as it is for the racers; the racing is challenging, high-velocity stuff on open coastal waters.

There are several different types of offshore racing:

- Class 3C (which has superceded the 2-litre class), Offshore Circuit racing and RIB racing (in Rigid Inflatable Boats) are all open series. These are exciting, allow choice in engines and boat design, and make a reasonable entry point for people looking to forward their career to greater heights.
- Honda Formula Four Stroke and V24 powerboat racing are one-design series with high performance boats. The race courses are close to shore and the noise blows the eardrums off the gripped spectators.

Power boating is about mixing speed with water, adding in a dash of danger, stirring in a slug of glamour and serving over a big engine. Its fast, it's furious and we love it! And it is oh so very *Miami Vice*.

GETTING INVOLVED

For the majority of power boating, the main thing you need is a love of speed and a strong stomach.

To get started in Thundercat racing, check out www.thundercatracing.co.uk and contact them directly to join the community. If you catch the bug, expect to pay from as little as £2500 for a second-hand start-up race package (this will include a boat, trailer and race kit); a new package will set you back around £6000.

For the other racing we've mentioned above, check out the following websites for further details:

Offshore racing:

- Zapcat Racing (www.zapcat-racing.com)
- Offshore Circuit Racing Drivers Association website (www.ocrda.org)
- Honda Formula 4 Stroke (www.honda-racing.co.uk/marine/hf4s)
- 3C (2-litre racing): visit the Offshore Racing Drivers Association website (www.orda.co.uk)
- Rib racing: visit www.biboa.com (British Inflatable Boat Owners' Association) and www.hotribs.com, the website for enthusiasts of rigid hull inflatable boats (RIBs) and inflatables
- V24 (www.v24powerboats.co.uk).

Circuit racing:

- Visit the Royal Yachting Association's (RYA) website for detailed information about circuit racing (www.rya.org.uk/Activities/Powerboat Racing/).

For all other power boat experiences, contact one of the companies or clubs we have listed below and try a one-off experience. (One off? – we don't think so. Prepare to be hooked!)

EQUIPMENT NEEDED

The equipment you need varies hugely depending on the type of power boat you want to ride and how far you would like to get involved. Again, check out the websites above and the list of clubs and companies below. Together, this should give you copious amounts of information about each sport in addition to full details of the equipment needed.

WHERE TO GET INVOLVED

ADMINISTRATIVE BODIES

Royal Yachting Association (RYA)
www.rya.org.uk
0845 345 0400
RYA House, Ensign Way, Hamble, Southampton, Hampshire SO31 4YA

The RYA is the UK's national association for all forms of recreational and competitive boating, including power boats.

CLUBS, SOCIETIES AND COMPANIES

South-east and London

Allhallows Yacht Club
www.ayc.uk.com
01634 270788

Bembridge Sailing Club
www.bembridgesailingclub.org
01983 872237

Dover Water Sports Centre
www.doverwatersports.com
01304 212880

Queen Mary Sailing Club
www.queenmary.org.uk
01784 248881

Rockley Watersports
www.rockleywatersports.com
0870 7770541

Thundercat Racing UK
www.thundercatracing.co.uk
0870 2207165

Zapcat Racing
www.zapcat-racing.com
02392 526000

WHERE TO GET INVOLVED

South-west

Penhale Adventure Centre
www.penhaleadventure.com
0800 781 6861

South Wales Lakes Trust
www.swlakestrust.org.uk
01566 771930

Torbay and Dartmouth Powerboat School
www.powerboat-instruction.co.uk
01803 855508

Wales and West Midlands

Croft Farm Waterpark
www.croftfarmleisure.co.uk
01684 772321

Edgbaston Watersports
www.edgbastonwatersports.co.uk
0121 4541997

The National Watersports Centre
www.plasmenai.co.uk
01248 673943

Pembrokeshire Activity Centre
www.pembrokeshire-activity-centre.co.uk
01646 622013

East Midlands

Carsington Sports and Leisure
www.carsingtonwater.com
01629 540478

Northampton Watersports Centre
www.northamptonwatersports.com
01604 880248

Rutland Watersports
www.anglianwaterleisure.co.uk
01780 460154

Northern England

Coquet Shorebase Trust
www.coquetshorebase.org.uk
01665 710367

North Lincolnshire and Humberside Sailing Club
www.nlsail.co.uk
01652 632514

Rother Valley Country Park
www.rothervalleycountrypark.co.uk
0114 2471452

Windermere Outdoor Adventure
www.southlakelandleisure.org.uk/windermere
015394 47183

Scotland

Jet Ski Ecosse
www.jetskiecosse.co.uk
01294 279977

Royal Forth Yacht Club
www.rfyc.org
0131 5528560

Scottish National Sports Centre Cumbrae
www.nationalcentrecumbrae.org.uk
01475 530757

Sea Skills
www.seaskills.co.uk
01620 895135 (after 6 pm)

Northern Ireland

Royal North of Ireland Yacht Club
www.rniyc.org
028 9042 8041

34 SURFING

WATER

BUZZ FOR YOUR BUCK 6/10
THRILL FACTOR

'I've been surfing for 21 years and have been British Champion six times, and I still get the same buzz now as I did when I started.'

***Lee Bartlett**, six-times British Surfing Champion*

Catching a wave, riding a barrel, looking suntanned and toned in a wetsuit . . . it's what the word 'cool' was invented for. But surfing's not just about looking cool (although photos of Adonis- and Aphrodite-like readers hitting the waves are always gratefully received here for the office pin board). Surfing is also about participating in an adrenaline-fuelled, addictive adventure sport while sharing your passion with thousands of fellow surfers.

Believe it or not, it was Hawaiian islanders in the 1400s who were busy developing this state of 'cool' when they invented he'e nalu, or 'wave sliding'. Spreading in the early twentieth century to mainland USA and Australia, wave sliders became 'surfers'. They used heavy timber boards until the development of cheaper, lighter boards made of fibreglass and foam in the 1960s. While land lubbers threw themselves into flower power and the Beatles, droves of water babies threw off their kaftans and took to the seas on these new boards – and the sport of surfing took off. Today, the popularity of the sport, in spite of competition from various newcomers on the adventure sports scene, shows no signs of abating.

The moves and styles of surfing are numerous, although riding barrels (sometimes called 'tubes') is probably surfing's holy grail. Even the most die-hard surfers dream of catching a wave just at the point it curls over them and experiencing the adrenaline-pounding ride through the tunnel of water.

Competitive surfing is hugely popular both with surfers and sponsors. It's arguably the latter's commercial desire to be associated with the sport and inject cash into it that helps raise the sport's profile even further. Typically, riders competing against each other have a certain amount of time to ride waves and display their prowess and mastery of the board. Judging is based on how competently the wave is ridden and the frequency (and complexity) of manoeuvres. Competitions are held regionally and nationally in the UK, with the Oscars of the surfing world being the international competitions held all over the globe.

Less well known, but growing in popularity, is big wave surfing, also known as big wave hunting. This involves riding the biggest waves possible. However, we should hastily point out that this experience isn't available in tamer UK waters. To catch the biggest waves, head for massive ocean swells off the coasts of Hawaii, California, South Africa, Mexico and Australia; dedicated surfers follow the world's winter storms to catch them. Big wave surfing involves surfers being towed out on jet skis to where they'll be able to catch the really big, fast-moving waves. Some of these waves reach speeds of 60km/h (38 mph) or more, so without jet skis surfers wouldn't stand a chance of catching them. The biggest wave ever ridden, we believe, remains the 21-metre (70-feet) wave ridden off the coast of Hawaii in 2004 (but, as always, do get in touch if you know of a bigger one). Big wave surfing is fast, dangerous, and given the distances out to sea, not exactly a spectator sport. The best way to see what it's all about is to watch footage of it – check out some awesome video clips on www.surfermap.com.

So, is surfing for you? Surfing is physically demanding; you'll need to be reasonably fit and a good swimmer (obviously). So, if you love the water and can handle its unpredictable nature, if you want the challenge of developing your board skills as you master cutbacks, floaters (not what you might think) and off-the-lip moves, and if you dream of riding a barrel, ripping the waves up and returning to the beach a hero or heroine, then surfing is most definitely for you.

GETTING INVOLVED

When starting to surf you need to master the basic techniques, such as how to catch a wave and stand on the board. Combine this with the vagaries of the sea and the importance of understanding currents and weather conditions to ensure safety, and we'd strongly recommend you take a few lessons to start with (the rules and code of conduct for surfing and bodyboarding can be found at www.britsurf.co.uk/html/code_of_conduct.asp.). How many lessons you need will depend on how quickly you pick it up – some people require only one or two days-worth, others need longer. The instructors teaching you will take you to a safe beach, with fewer hazards and people, and smaller user-friendly waves to start out on. They'll also give you invaluable advice on the etiquette of surfing, which is more about ensuring you surf safely around fellow surfers than holding your board the right way. If you choose a surf school that has been approved by the British Surfing Association – and we've listed some below – you'll be in good hands. Expect to pay around £30 for a half-day course, £50 for a full-day and £90 for a weekend.

TAKING IT FURTHER

There's really no limit to how far you can take surfing, from executing perfect manoeuvres for your own satisfaction, competing in the many competitions at club and national level (such as the British Interclub Surfing Championships and British National Surfing Championships), right through to hitting the international scene. At international level, you can aim for the World Qualifying Series, held all over the globe, the World Surfing Games or the ISA World Masters Surfing Championships. And then, of course, there's always the change-of-lifestyle option, which involves giving up your desk-bound job in the Big Smoke and becoming a full-time surfing instructor in Cornwall. . .

EQUIPMENT NEEDED

If you take lessons at surf school, you'll be able to hire all the kit you need. But once you're hooked you'll need to shoe-horn yourself into your own wetsuit and buy your own board. Generally, you'll want to wear a full-length wetsuit in colder waters and a 'shorty' (a wetsuit cut off at the knees and shoulders) for all those tropical days we're blessed with in the UK. Depending on the brand, expect to pay around £80–£100 for a basic full-length wetsuit (and up to £250 for some) and around £50 for a 'shorty'; there is also a very good second-hand market.

Now, for your surfboard. . . If you find choosing sweets from a pick 'n' mix selection a challenge, make sure you seek advice when buying a surfboard, as the selection can be mind-boggling. A standard surfboard (for more experienced surfers) measures around 1.93–2.05 m (6 ft 4 in–6 ft 10 in) long and 45–50 cm (18–20 in) wide, and weighs around 3.5 kg (8 lb). However, when you're starting out you will want a larger surfboard to give you more stability (when I started out I could have done with a board the size of the beach car park). But it's not as simple as just size, it's also about the many different designs of board: a shortboard (also known as a 'thruster'), The Fish, The Gun, Malibu . . . the choice is endless. Prices might start at around £180 and go up to £500 or more for custom-made boards.

Wax is also a key part of the surfer's kit, for two reasons (listed in order of importance):

1 Waxing a board is to surfers what going to the pub is for land lubbers (it allows you to stand around chatting to your mates) and has become an all-important surfing ritual.
2 Wax repels water and stops you slipping.

SURFING: A WHOLE NEW MEANING TO CATCHING THE TUBE. . .

Other surfing kit includes leashes, traction pads and interchangeable skegs, or fins, for your board. Take plenty of advice from seasoned surfers when buying any of the kit mentioned above. Surfing is a highly commercial business and it's easy to get swayed by all the branding and advertising.

WHERE TO GET INVOLVED

ADMINISTRATIVE BODIES

British Surfing Association (BSA) and British Bodyboarding Club (BBC)
www.britsurf.co.uk
01637 876474

The British Surfing Association and British Bodyboarding Club, The International Surfing Centre, Fistral Beach, Newquay, Cornwall TR7 1HY

The BSA and BBC is recognised by the Government as the national governing body for surfing and body boarding in the UK and is a member of the International Surfing Association (ISA).

CLUBS AND SOCIETIES

South-east and London

Shore Surf Club
www.shoresurfclub.co.uk
01243 514774

South-west

British Longboard Union
www.britishlongboardunion.co.uk
07970 955658

Croyde Surf Club
www.croydesurfclub.com
01271 817862

Hibiscus Surf School (women only)
www.hibiscussurfschool.co.uk
01637 879374

Hotdoggers Longboarding Club
www.hotdoggers.co.uk
01271 328489

St Agnes Surf Club
www.aggiesurfclub.co.uk
01209 890060

Watergate Bay Surf Club
www.thesurfclub.co.uk

Wales and West Midlands

Welsh Coast Surf Club
www.welshcoastsurf.com
07742 332558

East Anglia

East Anglia Surfing Association
www.eastcoastsurf.co.uk/EASA

East Coast Surf
www.eastcoastsurf.co.uk
01603 305511

Scotland

Granite City Surf Club
www.granitereef.com
01224-252752

Surf and Watersports Club
www.surfandwatersportsclub-scotland.com
01261 815228

35 WATER SKIING, WAKEBOARDING, HYDROFOILING

BUZZ FOR YOUR BUCK 8/10
THRILL FACTOR

Shoe-horn your tanned and toned body into a wetsuit, don your water skis, and let the speed boat pull you stylishly from the water like a sea god or goddess. Swing out wide behind the boat, hop casually back and forth over its wake, and wave nonchalantly as you skim past the admiring crowds on the beach . . . and then wake up. For many of us, our first attempts to water ski start with an arm-jerking heave out of the water, a wobble forward, and probably a nose dive back into the brine. However, this is a sport you can master relatively quickly.

Water skiing was invented in 1922 by Ralph Samuelson of Minnesota when he took to the water with his feet strapped on to the curved staves of barrels. This wasn't an entirely successful first attempt, but after many design modifications over the past 80 years, modern-day water skis have evolved into fibre-glass-based composites with rubber-moulded foot bindings.

The beauty of water skiing is not only the thrill of the speeds you can travel, but the challenge of the techniques you can learn and the tricks you can execute. Once you've learned to ski on two skis you might want to progress to using a single ski, placing one foot behind the other. As a beginner on two skis, you'll cruise along behind the speedboat at around 25–35 km/h (15–28 mph), but as a more seasoned mono-skier you'll be flying along at between 40 and 58 km/h (25–36 mph). Perhaps the ultimate water skiing challenge is barefoot skiing, which does exactly what it says on the tin. With your feet acting as the platform to lift you out of the water, the boat will pull you along even faster, at speeds of 43–65 km/h (27–40 mph).

As with all adventure sports, there are always enthusiasts willing to take the sport further and to new extremes – and water skiing is no exception. Wakeboarding and hydrofoiling have both been invented off the back of water skiing.

Wakeboarding

Wakeboarding is a cross between water skiing, snowboarding and surfing. It uses a single board (typically shorter and wider than a snowboard) with stationary non-release bindings for each foot. Stand sideways on the board and get ready to use the wake of the boat as ramps from which you launch

WAKEBOARDING: A FRONT FLIP, ELEPHANT OR HALF-CAB ROLL?

into tricks (often airborne) such as a Tantrum (a backflip), Elephant (similar to a move called the Scarecrow involving a 180 degree rotation in the air) and a Board Slide (where you lie back in the water).

Hydrofoiling

Hydrofoiling is another form of water skiing which has grown significantly in popularity. The main difficulty with this sport is describing the actual 'thing' you hydrofoil on. So, alert to the reality that we're going to have a postbag full of letters from people telling us we've explained it wrong, we're going to prep the postman for the onslaught and say: 'It's a board with a seat on it (although not always) with a foil (a vertical strut coming out of the bottom of the board that looks a bit like a model aeroplane attached to the end, but which is in fact a finely-tuned piece of engineering)'. Now, if that's confused you as much as we think it has, check out the many hydrofoiling websites that boast excellent diagrams (and write to us if you can describe it better).

One of the keys to hydrofoiling is the large distances you can cruise because, unlike water skiing, the foil is so streamlined and efficient that the amount of effort it takes to hold on to the rope is considerably less. Flying the hydrofoil above the water, you'll probably master jumps first and then progress on to flips and rolls. Prepare to get to heights of 7.6 metres (25 feet) as you master the skidder, MacThruster, rodeo, floater and flying chicken.

Water skiing is a hugely popular sport in the UK due to its speed, availability, fun and suitability for all ages and levels of experience, and this popularity shows no sign of abating. So, if you've never tried it, then it's time to get down to your nearest water skiing centre and get wet!

GETTING INVOLVED

Water ski tuition is a must for novices as otherwise, unless you are incredibly gifted, you'll simply get frustrated because you can't get out of the water. After a couple of sessions of good tuition – and there are plenty of clubs, schools and water sport centres throughout the UK offering this – you'll be up on the skis and starting to feel more relaxed. Expect to pay around £30–45 for an introductory 30-minute session.

Water skiing is a physically demanding sport, so each session will normally last no more than 15 minutes. Even frequent skiers struggle to ski more than three times in one day.

TAKING IT FURTHER

With nearly as many events in the calendar as premiership football, there are plenty of water ski competitions to get stuck into. Take your pick of UK tournament water skiing or step out in to the international arena for the European Championships, World Championships, World Cup, French Masters and Malibu Open. If you're not looking to take part in competitions but want to progress from straightforward water skiing, then clubs and schools will help you move on to mono-skiing, wakeboarding and the impossible-to-describe, but brilliant, hydrofoiling.

EQUIPMENT NEEDED

Water skiing is an easy sport to get started with because schools and centres will provide you with all the kit you need – a wetsuit, buoyancy aid, skis or wakeboard. So, all you'll need to bring for your first few outings are a swimsuit and towel. You'll also need the same basic equipment for wakeboarding, mono-skiing and hydrofoiling, although you may decide to buy some of your own kit when you move on to these. Once you get hooked and want to buy your own kit, the cost of new water skis and wake boards vary according to brand and design. Expect to pay a minimum £100 and anticipate spending more like £170 plus. However, you might want to check your bank balance before you go the whole hog and buy the speed boat.

MAKING HUGE WAVES – WATER SKIING

WHERE TO GET INVOLVED

ADMINISTRATIVE BODIES

British Water Ski Federation
www.britishwaterski.org.uk
01932 570885
British Water Ski, The Tower, Thorpe Road, Chertsey, Surrey KT16 8PH

British Water Ski is the National Governing Body for water skiing and wakeboarding in the UK.

CLUBS, SOCIETIES AND COMPANIES

South-east and London

British Water Ski National Site
www.britishwaterski.org.uk
01932 570885

Hi5 Water Ski & Wakeboard
www.hi5ski.co.uk
01189 394709

Princes Club
www.princesclub.com
01784 256153

Quayside Wakeboard and Water Ski
www.quaysws.co.uk
01252 524375

South-west

Camel Ski School
ww.camelskischool.com
01208 862727

Fairford Water Ski Club Ltd
www.craigcohoon.co.uk
01285 713735

Point Breaks
www.pointbreaks.com
07776 148679

Ski West Watersports
www.skiwest.co.uk
01803 663243

Weston Bay Water Sports Club
www.westonski.co.uk
01934 418377

Wales and West Midlands

Bomere Water Ski Club
www.bomere.co.uk
01743 872122

Deeside Water Ski Club
www.deesidewaterskiclub.org.uk
01244 821728

Dudley Water Ski Club
www.dudleywaterski.co.uk
01384 566250

Llangorse Water Ski Club
www.llwsc.com
07711 109876

Offaxis
www.offaxis.co.uk
01758 713407

Ten-80 Wakeboard and Water Ski
www.ten-80.co.uk
07813 300916

WHERE TO GET INVOLVED

Wakeboard UK
www.wakeboard.co.uk
01564 700309
East Midlands

Church Wilne Water Sports Club
www.churchwilne.co.uk
01332 875574

Hazelwood Ski World
www.malibuboats.co.uk
01522 688887

Northampton Water Ski Club
www.northamptonwaterski.co.uk
01604 709440

Skegness Cable Ski Centre
www.waterskiskeggy.co.uk
07889 243889

East of England
Tallington Lakes
www.tallington.com
01778 347000
E-mail: info@tallington.com

Northern England
National Water Sports Centre
www.nationalwatersportsevents.co.uk
0115 9824707.

Sheffield Cable Water Ski
www.sheffieldcablewaterski.com
0114 2511717

Whitworth Water Ski Centre
www.whitworth-waterski.co.uk
01706 852534

Yorkshire Water Ski Club
www.yorkshirewsc.freeserve.co.uk

Scotland
Aberdeen Water Ski Club
www.aberdeenwaterski.info
01224 783948

Kyle Water Ski Club
www.kylewaterskiclub.org.uk
01505 842868

Loch Lomond Water Ski Club
www.lochlomondwaterskiclub.co.uk
01436 860632

Water Ski Scotland
www.waterskiscotland.co.uk
01383 620123

Northern Ireland
Ultimate Watersports
www.ultimatewatersports.co.uk
07808 736818

36 WHITE WATER RAFTING

BUZZ FOR YOUR BUCK 8/10
THRILL FACTOR 8/10

So, you thought white water rafting was just an afternoon's 'filler' on a stag or hen do, huh? Well, think again. The International Rafting Federation (IRF) presides over a whole raft (pardon the pun) of national and international competitions. Take your pick from the World Rafting Championships, European Rafting Championships and a whole series of Cup competitions in countries across the globe, but just be sure to adhere to the competition standards and policies set by the IRF or you'll find yourself up the proverbial creek with not a paddle in sight. But before you set your sights on reaching international competition standard, white water rafting makes a great day out for a group of friends who want to get wet, scream for Britain, and arrive back on dry land buzzing from the adrenaline rush of tearing down rapids.

Rafting is very much a team sport with, typically, between four and eight people in what's normally about a 4.3-metre (14-foot) inflatable raft. Before you take to the waters you'll be given full instructions on safety, where to sit in the raft and how to paddle. Then you'll be taken to the launch site and, with an experienced guide at the back of the raft, you'll set off on your first run of the course. Your guide will act as the steering wheel, calling out instructions to you while you paddle like hell as the 'engine'. Not all the time is going to be spent whooshing down rapids – there'll be a lot of paddling on flat water, and bumping and gliding down the river's course, to get to them. But this is time for banter before you hit the rapids screaming with excitement and exhilaration.

As long as you're over the minimum age set by the individual white water rafting centre, reasonably, physically fit, confident in water and like a wet, white-knuckle ride, then rafting is for you (however, some centres may have other restrictions, so do check ahead). Many people get the bug and go on to become guides or join teams and take part in the various white water rafting competitions. The beauty of this adventure sport is that it doesn't need hours of patient practice before you're enjoying it to its full potential – in just one afternoon you can be out on the water and having the time of your life.

GETTING INVOLVED

There are many, many companies around the UK where you can experience half a day of rafting fun for around £50 per person. In some places, you will

WHITE WATER RAFTING: IT'S ALL ABOUT TEAMWORK

only to be able to raft when water levels are high enough – this typically tends to be between October and May each year, so do check with companies where they operate white water rafting.

EQUIPMENT NEEDED

Centres offering white water rafting will provide you with all the equipment you need; generally, a wetsuit, wetsuit jacket, buoyancy aid, helmet, gloves, boots and socks. All you need to take along is some swimwear, a long-sleeved top and a towel. You should also make sure that you have some warm, dry clothes to change into afterwards.

WHERE TO GET INVOLVED

ADMINISTRATIVE BODIES

British Canoe Union (BCU)
www.bcu.org.uk
0115 982 1100
British Canoe Union HQ, John Dudderidge House, Adbolton Lane, West Bridgford, Nottingham NG2 5AS

The BCU is the lead body for canoeing, kayaking and white water rafting in the UK. The International Rafting Federation (based in the USA) presides over the sport at an international level.

English White Water Rafting Committee (EWWRC)
The EWWRC is a sub-committee of the BCU and can be contacted through the BCU at the numbers above.

International Rafting Federation
www.intraftfed.com
00 1 27 217128503

Scottish Rafting Association
www.scottish-rafting-association.org.uk

The SRA is the lead body for white water rafting in Scotland.

Welsh Canoeing Association (and National Whitewater Centre)
www.welsh-canoeing.org.uk
01678 521083

COMPANIES

South-west

Penhale Adventure Centre
www.penhaleadventure.com
0800 781 6861

Wales and West Midlands

JJ Canoeing and Rafting
www.jjraftcanoe.com
01978 860763

WHERE TO GET INVOLVED

National Whitewater Centre
www.ukrafting.co.uk
01678 521083

Shaggy Sheep Wales
www.shaggysheepwales.co.uk
01267 281202

East Midlands

Nene Whitewater Centre
www.nenewhitewatercentre.co.uk
01604 634040

Northern England

National Water Sports Centre
www.nationalwatersportsevents.co.uk
0115 9824707

Teeside White Water Centre
www.4seasons.co.uk
01642 678000

Scotland

Activ8s
www.activ8s.com
01887 830292

Dunolly Adventures
www.dunollyadventures.co.uk
01887 820298

Freespirits
www.freespirits-online.co.uk
0845 6444755

Nae Limits
www.naelimits.co.uk
01350 727242

Splash White Water Rafting
www.rafting.co.uk

Wild Spirits
www.wildspirits.co.uk
0870 760 7582

HOLD ON TO YOUR HELMETS AS YOU HIT THE TUMBLING RAPIDS!

37

WINDSURFING

BUZZ FOR YOUR BUCK 6/10
THRILL FACTOR ▮▮▮▮▮▮□□□□

Picture this: you're standing on a podium being watched by thousands in the arena and millions of TV viewers around the world. The national anthem is playing. You lift your gold medal to the sky and kiss it. You've become an international sporting star and you're going to return home a national hero. Sound good? Then get down to your nearest windsurfing centre and you could be on your way to Olympic stardom. . . Think we're day dreaming? Well, the picture is much closer to reality than you might think. Brits have proved that they're really rather good at windsurfing.

- Nick Dempsey brought home a bronze medal from the Athens Olympics in 2004.
- The current Windsurfing World Speed Record is held by Irish-born Finian Maynard, who reached a speed of 90 km/h (48.7 knots) in 2005.
- In April 2006, British teenager Richard Jones became the fastest and youngest person to windsurf across the Channel, crossing in just 1 hour 14 minutes.

- Many people argue that the sport was invented by a Brit named Peter Chilvers, who developed his craft in 1958.

The popularity of windsurfing grows annually and, based on requests made by passengers on spectator boats at the Sydney Olympic Regatta, windsurfing was one of the top three regularly requested events to watch. Although it is difficult to know exactly how many people windsurf, statistics lead us to believe there were 20 million worldwide in 2004, and the figure will have grown since then. Sometimes the fastest sailing craft afloat (Irish windsurfer Finian Maynard set a World Speed Sailing Record in 2005 when he reached an average speed of 48.7 knots (56.05 mph) over a 500-metre (0.3-mile) course), windsurfers provide us with everything from racing on flat water and wave riding in competitions to the sheer pleasure of taking to inland lakes and seas for fun. Windsurfing is relatively easy to start and, as a sport represented by the Royal Yachting Association (RYA), there are places all over the UK where you can either take part in training courses or simply have a go.

THE POPULARITY OF WINDSURFING KEEPS ON GROWING

Boards have developed through sophisticated design from the huge, heavy plastic objects of the 1980s, which has resulted in smaller, lighter boards and an infinitely better sail. As a beginner, you'll start on a larger board to help stability and, typically, your sail may be smaller so that it catches less wind and is easier to heave out of the water. The beauty of learning to windsurf is that it won't be long before you're up and windsurfing – using modern kit with its increased stability helps make this process much quicker. However, it may take a lot more practice and patience to experience the real thrill of windsurfing – planing. This is the moment when the board goes from floating along in the water to skimming along on top of it. The adrenaline rush of this is incredible. From then on you'll be ready to learn to harness, waterstart, carve (alter your course at high speed by banking the board like a ski) and duck gybe (an advanced turn or 'gybe', when you allow the sail to pass overhead rather than out to the front of the board) . . . and by now you'll be well and truly addicted.

An addiction to windsurfing may result in you wanting to take part in the many windsurfing events and competitions scheduled throughout the year in the UK. Some events last just 1 day, some a weekend, and some, such as

national championships, can last a week. Events might also be part of a series, where points from each event count towards the overall title. There are four main types of competition:

- *course racing* – a technical competition similar to dinghy sailing
- *wave sailing* – competing to perform the best tricks and rides on waves in front of a panel of judges
- *slalom* – high, straight speed and tight turns down zig-zag or Figure-of-eight courses
- *freestyle* – incredible tricks at low speeds and on flat waters.

And then there's indoor windsurfing. While this might sound as though it's designed for indoor wimps, it is in fact classed as an extreme sport. High-power fans create the wind for slalom races and these are followed by jumping competitions off a ramp lowered into the water. It's extreme because some competitors jump right out of the pool!

So, set your sights on having some fun at a windsurfing centre near you. Who knows, we may be in the party welcoming you home as you return from the Olympics a national hero. . .

GETTING INVOLVED

There's a whole raft of places you can go to learn to windsurf: sailing clubs, windsurfing clubs, watersports centres. The Royal Yachting Association (RYA) presides over the courses and qualifications, and affiliated clubs and centres will usually offer the National Windsurfing Scheme; this comprises:

- the RYA Start Windsurfing course
- the RYA Intermediate Windsurfing course (non-planing)
- the RYA Intermediate Windsurfing course (planing)
- the RYA Advanced Windsurfing course.

When you really get the bug and want to teach the National Windsurfing Scheme, a series of instructor courses will take you from assistant instructor through to senior instructor.

EQUIPMENT NEEDED

When you're starting out, the club or school you learn with will hire out the equipment you need. But it probably won't be long before you want to buy your own wetsuit and even windsurf. Windsurfers aren't prohibitively expensive – prices vary, but you can expect to pay around £800 for a new board and about £600 for a rig. There's also a good second-hand market. Your initial problem when buying your own rig will be deciding what to buy – there's a huge choice out there – so take plenty of advice from fellow windsurfing enthusiasts.

WHERE TO GET INVOLVED

ADMINISTRATIVE BODIES

Royal Yachting Association (RYA)
www.rya.org.uk
0845 345 0400
RYA House, Ensign Way, Hamble, Southampton, Hampshire SO31 4YA

The RYA is the UK's national association for all forms of recreational and competitive boating, including windsurfing.

UK Windsurfing Association
www. ukwindsurfing.com

CLUBS, SOCIETIES AND COMPANIES

South-east and London

Bewl Windsurfing
www.bewlwindsurfing.co.uk
01892 891000

Bognor Regis Yacht Club
www.bryc.co.uk
01243 865735

Dover Water Sports Centre
www.doverwatersports.com
01304 212880

Queen Mary Sailing Club
www.queenmary.org.uk
01784 248881

X-Train
www.x-train.co.uk
01243 513077

South-west

Penhale Adventure Centre
www.penhaleadventure.com
0800 781 6861

South West Lakes Trust
www.swlakestrust.org.uk
01566 771930

Waterfront Sports
www.waterfront-sports.co.uk
01395 276599

WHERE TO GET INVOLVED

Wales and West Midlands

Croft Farm Waterpark
www.croftfarmleisure.co.uk
01684 772321

Edgbaston Watersports
www.edgbastonwatersports.co.uk
0121 4541997

The National Watersports Centre
www.plasmenai.co.uk
01248 673943

Pembrokeshire Activity Centre
www.pembrokeshire-activity-centre.co.uk
01646 622013

East Midlands

Carsington Sports and Leisure
www.carsingtonwater.com
01629 540478

Northampton Watersports Centre
www.northamptonwatersports.com
01604 880248

Nottinghamshire County Sailing Club
www.ncsc.org.uk
01636 830065

Rutland Watersports
www.anglianwaterleisure.co.uk
01780 460154

East of England

Brogborough Boardsailing Club
www.brogboroughlake.co.uk
01234 768841

Northern England

Coquet Shorebase Trust
www.coquetshorebase.org.uk
01665 710367

North Lincolnshire and Humberside Sailing Club
www.nlsail.co.uk
01652 632514

Rother Valley Country Park
www.rothervalleycountrypark.co.uk
0114 2471452

Southport Boardsurfing Association
www.sbawindsurfing.org.uk
01772 814939

Surfstore
www.surfstore.co.uk
01740 631199

Windermere Outdoor Adventure
www.southlakelandleisure.org.uk/windemere
015394 47183

Scotland

Clyde Windsurfing Club
www.clydewindsurfing.co.uk
01505 842955

Scottish National Sports Centre Cumbrae
www.nationalcentrecumbrae.org.uk
01475 530757

UP FOR THE CHALLENGE

Do you have a competitive streak and are you up for a challenge? If so, read on. This section provides you with some information on the UK's ultimate challenges. You may not get the ultimate adrenalin buzz while competing, but the sense of achievement as you cross the finish line will give you an unforgettable high and some great memories – as well as a small trophy – that will be with you for the rest of your life. And if that's not enough, many of these events raise hundreds of thousands of pounds for charity so you have an opportunity to raise money for a good cause.

Challenges stretch from the South Coast of England to the North of Scotland and will test your endurance to the limit. They're not called challenges for nothing – if you complete them you'll be up there with the best.

We've listed some challenges here, but if you've done others and think people should know about them, send the details to us and we'll include them next time and on our website.

ARTEMIS GREAT KINDROCHIT QUADRATHALON: LOCH TAY, SCOTLAND

Arguably Scotland's toughest 1-day event, incorporating swimming, walking, running, kayaking and cycling. Held in July, it takes the most adventurous of us over and around Loch Tay and the summits of Ben Lawers Range and

Ptarmigan Ridge on a testing 13-hour, 96-km (60-mile) challenge. This one isn't for the amateur, but then what's a challenge without a challenge? Check out www.eventsandactivities.co.uk/grtkin.htm.

ARTEMIS HIGHLAND 100 CHALLENGE: LOCH TAY AND SURROUNDING AREA, SCOTLAND

This is a 12-hour challenge, which takes participants through over 100 km (62 miles) of some of the most spectacular and historical regions of the Highlands. Starting at Kenmore, teams head north towards the famous Schiehallion Munro and then southwest to Loch Rannoch, with stunning views out towards Rannoch Moor and beyond. The Artemis Highland 100 has been designed for the entire family to take part. See www.eventsandactivities.co.uk.

THE BALLBUSTER DUATHALON: BOX HILL, SURREY

The Ballbuster is aptly named, although some women do enter! If you've ever tried to walk, run or cycle up Box Hill, then you'll know why. This event takes you over Box Hill, near Dorking in Surrey, a total of five times. Each circuit is 12.8-km (8-miles) long and each lap finishes with the punishing climb to the finish. Two laps are completed on foot and three in the saddle; and no, not a horse – that would be way too easy. This is the equivalent of running a marathon with some challenging climbs, so it should be treated with the utmost respect. You won't be surprised to hear that many competitors don't make it to the finish line each year. This event is run in November, so the weather conditions can be variable. To find out more about The Ballbuster Duathlon check out www.humanrace.co.uk/buster/index.

THE CALEDONIAN CHALLENGE: FORT WILLIAM, LOCH LOMOND, SCOTLAND

The Caledonian Challenge does exactly what it says on the tin. It challenges you across 86 km (54 miles) of some of the best scenery in Scotland. The course starts just outside Fort William and takes you through Kinlochleven, over the Devils Staircase into Glencoe, across Rannoch Moor and on to the bonny banks of Loch Lomond (which might at that point feel less bonny than when you last saw them from the comfort of a car). The event is open to teams, and each team must have a minimum of three contestants. It is mainly a walking event, but some teams do run the distance. The course must be completed within 24 hours, and there is an excellent support infrastructure offered at four stations along the route. Find out more at www.caledonianchallenge.com.

THE TEN TORS CHALLENGE: DARTMOOR, ENGLAND

This challenges has been running since 1959 when 203 boys and girls tried it. The event has grown significantly over the years and is now limited to 2400 individuals (400 teams of six teenagers). The event takes place over a weekend in May as teams attempt to complete hikes of 56, 72 or 88 km (35, 45 or 55 miles) between ten nominated Tors, depending on competitors' age and ability. The event takes place over 2 days and the intention is that the teams should be self-sufficient, carrying everything they need to survive for 2 days on the Moor. Find out more at www.events.ex.ac.uk/tentors.

MAGGIE'S MONSTER BIKE AND HIKE: GREAT GLEN WAY, SCOTLAND

This annual event takes teams right across Scotland from Fort William in the West to Inverness in the East, along the Great Glen, Loch Ness and the Caledonian Canal. You have just 24 hours to cover the 113 km (70 miles) through a mixture of cycling and walking. See www.eventsandactivities.co.uk.

THE ROB ROY CHALLENGE: THE TROSSACHS, SCOTLAND

This is a new event that was first run in June 1996 and covers 88 km (55 miles) of the spectacular Rob Roy Way. It can be either a team or individual event and will provide anyone who is brave enough to go it alone with a tall challenge. To start, you will be faced with a 25-km (16-mile) walk/run from Drymen, near Loch Lomond, northeast through The Trossachs to Callander. You then switch to a mountain bike for a 63-km (39-mile) cycle ride, which takes you through Balquhidder to Kenmore on the banks of Loch Tay. Find out more at www.robroychallenge.com.

THE HIGHLAND CROSS: KINTAIL – BEAULY, SCOTLAND

The Highland Cross is exactly that; you traverse the spectacular Scottish Highlands from west to east, from Kintail through Glen Affric and Strathglass to Beauly.

Entry to the Highland Cross is by invitation only for 220 teams of three, but all athletic abilities are welcome. Once entries are in, the organisers decide who will be selected to take part – it is an honour to get a place in the race. So stop lounging around reading this book and log on now to www.highlandcross.co.uk to get your entry in.

THE NDCS THREE PEAKS CHALLENGE: BEN NEVIS – SNOWDON, SCOTLAND, ENGLAND AND WALES

The classic mountain challenge, which involves climbing the highest mountains in Scotland, England and Wales respectively, in 24 bone crunchingly, blister wincing, muscle stiffening hours.

You'll need to have between five and seven walkers at the start of each mountain, plus two drivers per vehicle. The event starts on a Saturday afternoon at the foot of Ben Nevis in Scotland, moving overnight to Scafell Pike in the Lake District, and then finally on to Snowdon in North Wales, before a dinner reception and party on the Sunday evening. Driving time is fixed at 10 hours and isn't included in your clocked walking time.

Ouch. Just writing about this one makes me want to reach for the muscle soak bath bubbles. . . Find out more at www.ndcschallenges.org.uk.

INDEX